Goes Down *Easy*

Recipes to help you cope *with* the challenge of eating during cancer treatment

Elise Mecklinger *with* the Princess Margaret Hospital Dietitians

The Princess Margaret Hospital Foundation

University Health Network

The Princess Margaret Hospital Foundation would like to thank the Princess Margaret Hospital Breast Centre Women's Committee for funding this project.

Canadian Cataloguing in Publication Data ISBN 0-9780496-0-8

Mecklinger, Elise
Goes down easy : recipes to help you cope with the challenge of eating during cancer treatment Elise Mecklinger with the Princess Margaret Hospital dietitians.

Includes bibliographical references and index.

1. Cancer--Diet therapy--Recipes.
I. Princess Margaret Hospital Foundation II. Title.

RC268.45.M42 2006   641.5'631   C2006-901818-9

Art Directors/Designers (Volunteer): Gillian Tsintziras/Chris Tsintziras
Photographer (Volunteer): Edward Pond (www.edwardpond.com)
Food Stylist (Volunteer): Nicole Young
Book Editor (Volunteer): Arlene Gryfe
Recipe Editor (Volunteer): Barb Holland
Nutrient Analysis: Barbara Selley, Food Intelligence Inc.
Printing and Binding: University of Toronto Press Inc.

Front cover photograph: Tofu Tiramisù, page 130
Back cover photograph: Vanilla Cupcakes, page 70

To order your "Goes Down Easy" cookbook:
Online: visit www.pmhf.ca and go to the Online Store link or
go directly to http://pmhf.uhnstore.ca and go to View Products
By Phone: Call 1-866-YES-PMHF (1-866-937-7643) or 416-946-6560

The Princess Margaret Hospital Foundation
700 University Avenue, 8th Floor
Toronto, ON Canada M5G 1Z5

Charitable Organization No. 88900 7597 RR001

Thank you for your support to Help Conquer Cancer!

In memory of
Arthur Konviser and Monica Wright Roberts
in admiration of their personal commitment
to improve the lives of people living with cancer.

Dear Friends and Supporters:

On behalf of The Princess Margaret Hospital Foundation I am pleased to have the opportunity to offer you this very practical and unique cancer resource. The idea for this cookbook came about as so many good ideas often do when friends put their heads together. During an aerobics class in the fall of 2003 I ran into Elise Mecklinger, a friend and experienced cookbook author. During our conversation I asked her if she would consider donating her time to write a cookbook for cancer patients to raise funds for Princess Margaret Hospital. Shortly after, we approached the Foundation with this idea and as the saying goes "the rest is history".

Research confirmed that while a number of cancer cookbooks focus on cancer prevention and healthy eating, there are few cancer books specifically geared towards helping people and their families living with cancer to address dietary concerns as they move through the various stages of treatment – surgery, radiation, chemotherapy, post-treatment and recovery. It is estimated that every year 149,000 Canadians will be diagnosed with some form of cancer. We know that eating well during cancer treatment can be challenging. Forty to eighty percent of cancer patients experience nutritional deterioration during the course of their disease and 20% of cancer-related deaths are attributable to malnutrition.

Elise Mecklinger worked closely with a team of six registered dietitians at Princess Margaret Hospital, led by Daniela Fierini, to develop the recipes for *Goes Down Easy*. The book addresses the most common cancer side effects – loss of appetite, nausea, taste changes, swallowing difficulties, and diarrhea.

Proceeds from the sale of this book go to The Princess Margaret Hospital Foundation to support nutrition and patient education programs at the hospital. For more information on the activities of the Foundation or to purchase a copy of the book online, visit www.pmhf.ca and go to the Online Store link or call 416-946-6560 or 1-866-937-7643.

I would personally like to thank all the people who contributed their time and talents to make this cookbook possible, especially my dear friend, Elise Mecklinger.

Carole Grafstein, CM
Volunteer Chair, Princess Margaret Hospital Breast Centre
Women's Committee Board Member,
The Princess Margaret Hospital Foundation

ACKNOWLEDGEMENTS

From The Princess Margaret Hospital Foundation

The Princess Margaret Hospital Foundation would like to thank the amazing team of people who worked on *Goes Down Easy: Recipes to help you cope with the challenge of eating during cancer treatment.* We had no idea that such a large number of talented individuals would be involved and so many of you would so generously volunteer your time and wisdom. We would like to thank each and every one of you for "hanging in there" with us to complete this book and for your many special contributions.

Carole Grafstein, Volunteer Chair of the Princess Margaret Hospital (PMH) Breast Centre Women's Committee for initiating this project, and her Committee for agreeing to fund this publication, with proceeds from the 2005 Laugh Lines comedy event.

Elise Mecklinger, author, editor and publisher of a number of cookbooks for charity, who donated her time and talents to develop the recipes and guide us with her expertise and advice.

The Princess Margaret Hospital registered dietitians: Daniela Fierini, Susan Haines, Danielle Himel, Betty Lemon, Janis Winocur, and Connie Giordano Ziembicki who worked with Elise to ensure that the ingredients for every recipe were appropriate for each cancer symptom chapter and for their contributions to the introduction, dietary information, meal plans, and appendix.

Daniela Fierini for her outstanding commitment to this project – for showcasing this book to other professionals, helping the Foundation oversee this project, assisting with numerous testings and tastings, contributing to the text of the book, putting together the typed manuscript, and making all content revisions.

Audrey Jusko Friedman, Director of Patient Education and Survivorship at PMH for coming up with the concept for the book and helping us promote the book to patients and families as well as cancer centres in Ontario and across the country.

Kathie Baggett, Research Officer at The Princess Margaret Hospital Foundation who completed research on the cancer cookbook market for us.

Barb Holland, Freelance Home Economist and Food Writer for being our chief recipe editor and for providing us with her excellent expertise and advice.

Marian Macdonald, retired Kraft Kitchens Senior Manager for coordinating the recipe editing and testing with a larger group of professional Home Economists and for sharing her wealth of experience with us.

The Home Economists who volunteered their time to test every recipe in the book: Julia Aitken, Teresa Black, Carol Ann Brown, Mary Buncic, Margaret Fraser, Linda Hodgkinson, Barb Holland, Olga Kaminskyj, Euphemia London, Kera Pesall, Judy

Pohlmann, Marian Macdonald, Kathleen Mackintosh, Sue Quirt, Adele Rogers, Yvonne Tremblay, Lois Turk and Sandy Whitehouse.

Scott Secord for coordinating a recipe tasting with cancer survivors at Gilda's Club in Toronto.

Helen Hatton, Home Economist and Food Writer for putting us in contact with her wonderful network of food professionals and for coordinating the team of professionals that prepared and served the recipes for the tasting conducted at Gilda's Club: Cheryl Topitsch and Michelle Wolfson who were the chief volunteer chefs, and the team of volunteers who assisted them: Paula Bambrick, Juanita Costa, Melanie Green, Tammy Fansabedian (Princess Margaret Hospital Dietetic Intern), Zoe Cormack Jones, Debbi Moses, Glenda Towne (Princess Margaret Hospital Diet Technician), Kathy Wazana, and Anita Whyte.

Recipe tasters at Gilda's Club: Beth Beeley, Richard Brown, Gina Cali, Anthony Cammareri, Carmel Derdaele, Judy Granville, Patricia Hadzalic, Tina Norton, Ruth Page, David Raponi-Monk, Lorna Rosenstein, Charlotte Schultz, Scott Secord, and Lydia Young.

Barbara Selley of Food Intelligence Inc. who completed the nutrition analysis.

Arlene Gryfe of Gryfe Health Services Consultants Inc. for her tireless work editing the cookbook.

Jean Wheeler of J & F Wheeler Associates who compiled the index.

Gillian Tsintziras and Chris Tsintziras, art directors and designers of our book.

Edward Pond who created our artistic food photography shots in his studio; Jan Bird his representative who helped coordinate the shoot; and Nicole Young, the food stylist who made our recipes look fantastic.

Reg Hunt of the University of Toronto Press Inc. for printing and binding the first edition of our book.

Ryerson nutrition students: Puja Bansal, Abigail Brodovitch, Melinda Figliano, Kathryn Hall, Anjali Sambhi, and Linda Stoyanoff who volunteered their time to either help with the recipe tips or the appendix of the book.

Shelley Kamin, Barrister and Solicitor for her valuable legal counsel and advice, as she donated many hours of her time to us.

Shannon Doherty who acted as project coordinator on behalf of The Princess Margaret Hospital Foundation and without whose dedication and enthusiasm this project would not have become a reality.

To everyone who purchases *Goes Down Easy*, we sincerely hope that it helps you cope better with eating challenges you or your loved one experience during cancer treatment.

INTRODUCTION

The dietitians at Princess Margaret Hospital, Toronto, Canada are proud to be involved in this project with Elise Mecklinger. We were inspired by our patients' requests for easy, practical recipes to deal with certain nutrition problems they were experiencing. This has been a great opportunity to be part of a team to create a useful resource for people going through treatment, their caregivers and health care professionals alike.

Goes Down Easy is designed for people living with cancer, as well as their families and friends. Many people have to cope with illness and treatment that affect their ability to eat. This cookbook provides practical ideas on how to increase your intake during challenging times. Each chapter contains recipes that deal with a specific nutrition issue, and begins with practical tips on managing that problem. Also, there is a sample menu in each chapter, to help with meal planning and to make it easy to find appropriate recipes when you need them.

This book can be used at any point during your cancer experience, whether it is at diagnosis, during treatment or after treatment is finished. You may not need every chapter, because you are unlikely to experience every nutrition problem. You may find that some of the strategies work for you and others do not. Take advantage of any suggestions that help. The appendices at the back of the book provide information on:

- where to find ingredients
- how to stock your pantry
- what is a healthy diet
- food safety
- tips for meeting your fluid needs.

There may be times when you are unable to achieve a balanced diet, and that is okay. One goal of nutrition during cancer treatment is to maintain your weight and strength. Another goal is to keep well hydrated. The focus of your nutrition plan when you are having trouble eating is to have enough calories, protein and fluid. This book will help you to meet these goals. When you have completed treatment and are feeling well, you may want to make some lifestyle changes. Take a look at Chapter 6 – *Getting Back on Track*, which provides information on making the shift to long-term healthy eating.

A NOTE ON FATIGUE

The most common problem that people mention during cancer treatment is feeling extremely tired. This alone can make it difficult to eat well. Fatigue can prevent a person from shopping, cooking *and* eating. And don't even think of doing the dishes! The recipes in this book are geared to be simple, using just a few ingredients and requiring a small amount of preparation time. Many recipes can be frozen, so that when your energy is good, you can make a large batch to freeze for low-energy days. Remember, you don't have to do everything yourself. This is a great time to have family and friends help out. They are probably looking for ways to make your life easier. When they ask how they can help, why not give them a recipe from this book to make for you?

A NOTE FOR CAREGIVERS

If you do not know your way around a kitchen but are now in charge of preparing meals for your loved one, we hope that this cookbook will be a good resource for you.

We also want you to remember that your loved one may not always be able to eat what you prepare. Don't take it personally – their symptoms can change very quickly and so can their cravings. They still will appreciate what you are able to do for them.

Don't forget to ask for help for yourself! This can be a huge change in your life as well. Reach out to family and friends. They need you to tell them what they can do for you. Give them the chance to help you out.

A NOTE ON FOOD SAFETY

During times of illness, food safety becomes very important. Each recipe includes proper storage information. For more information on how to keep food safe from the grocery store to your home and to the table, please refer to the information in Appendix IV.

ABOUT THE NUTRIENT ANALYSIS FOR THE RECIPES

Nutrient values for the recipes were calculated by Food Intelligence Inc. with the assistance of Genesis® R & D Nutritional Analysis Program. The primary database was the Canadian Nutrient File. Calculations were based on:

- imperial ingredient quantities except when a metric amount would typically be purchased and used;
- first ingredient listed when there was a choice;
- smaller ingredient amount if there was a range; and
- smaller number of servings (larger portion) if there was a range.

Unless otherwise specified 2% milk and 1% yogurt were used in the calculations. Optional ingredients were not included.

Nutrient values have been rounded to the nearest whole number.

A NOTE ABOUT CROSSOVER RECIPES

There are a number of recipes in the book that are suitable for more than one chapter. In order to provide you with the widest selection of recipes for the problem you may be experiencing, we have included a list of *Crossover Recipes* after the *Recipe Index* at the start of each chapter.

The dietitians at Princess Margaret Hospital have enjoyed contributing to this book, and we hope that you find it helpful.

Daniela Fierini, Project Co-ordinator
Susan Haines, Danielle Himel, Betty Lemon, Janis Winocur, Connie Giordano Ziembicki

TABLE OF CONTENTS

CHAPTER 1

Loss *of* Appetite

Introduction

"I used to go for seconds, now I can't even finish what is on my plate."

Loss of appetite is a common concern for many people who have cancer and are undergoing treatment. Sometimes it is not so much a loss of appetite as a feeling of fullness after eating a very small amount. The stress of the diagnosis, the effect of the treatment on your body, and fatigue can also affect your appetite. Whatever the case, you may worry that you are not getting the nutrients your body needs to keep up your strength. Don't despair – there are ways you can boost your intake without it being an overwhelming task.

First of all, say *goodbye* to 3 meals a day and no snacks. Nibbling on small amounts every 1 to 2 hours may be a lot easier than sitting down to a large helping of food. Many people refer to this as "grazing." This chapter is designed to provide you with a number of "mini-meal" ideas to get you started.

Next, *make every mouthful count!* Go for the high-calorie and high-protein foods first. You will notice that every recipe in this chapter provides you with good quality protein and lots of calories.

Take a look at what you drink throughout the day. Do you have water or diet drinks with your meals? If so, replace them with juice or milk whenever you can. It is amazing how many calories you can add by simply making this switch.

Your appetite can come and go and so can your energy. It is a good idea to have some already prepared foods on hand that can be popped into the microwave or eaten directly out of the freezer. Most of the recipes in this chapter are quick and easy to prepare, use few ingredients and freeze well. You may decide to make a few on a day you have lots of energy or you can ask family and friends to stock up your freezer with some of your favourites.

HELPFUL HINTS FOR YOU

- Take snacks with you when you are away from home for periods of time because of treatment or doctor's appointments.
- Use dessert plates instead of dinner plates. Smaller portions are easier to tackle. If you are still hungry, go for seconds.
- Keep ready-made snack items in easy reach. Trail mix, cheese and crackers, pudding and ice cream are a few ideas for your shopping list.
- Go for a short walk in the neighbourhood. A little exercise and fresh air might stimulate your appetite.
- If you feel too tired to eat, take a few minutes to rest before mealtime.
- Listen to your body. Do you seem to have a better appetite in the morning or later in the day? If it is in the morning, have a hearty breakfast and then snack on some smaller items in the afternoon and evening.
- Distract yourself while you eat. Watch TV, listen to the radio, read a book, call a friend or play a game. It is surprising how many calories you can sneak in before you notice.
- Mix it up …have breakfast for dinner or dinner for breakfast – whatever works for you. It still provides good nutrition.
- If there are no pangs of hunger, it may be helpful to schedule your snacks just like you would schedule your medication. You may not want to think of food in this way but it might help for a short period of time.
- Satisfy cravings. It can wake up your appetite.

HELPFUL HINTS FOR THE CAREGIVER

- Spend a little time attractively arranging the food on the plate. Something that is pleasing to the eye may be easier to eat.
- Examine the environment. Soft lighting, a new tablecloth, pretty plates and relaxing music may make it more enjoyable to dine.
- As concerned as you may be, try not to force your loved one to eat. This can make a small appetite disappear very quickly.
- Make food easily available – a tin of nuts on the coffee table, a few peanut butter cookies at the bedside, a portable refrigerator filled with favourites next to a couch.
- Pleasant aromas may stimulate the appetite. For example, freshly baked bread, simmering stews, roasted vegetables or grilled foods. Make sure the aromas are not overpowering, as this will have the opposite effect.

How to Modify a Meal Plan

Protein and Calories

If you are losing weight because you have no appetite, here are examples of how to add protein and calories into your day without needing to eat a lot more food.

The extra protein you take in will help the body repair itself. Treatment may affect some of your normal tissue and protein is the only nutrient that can help with healing.

The extra calories you take in will help provide your body with energy. This energy will help to keep up your strength so that you can make it through treatment. The extra calories also mean that protein is less likely to be used for fuel by the body. Instead the body can use protein to heal and repair itself.

> Did you know…there are 3500 calories in 1 pound?
> By eating an extra 500 calories every day for 1 week, one could gain 1 lb!
> By eating an extra 500 calories every day for 1 month, one could gain 4 lb.

IS THIS HEALTHY?

If you are unable to maintain your weight, this may be the best way of eating for a short period of time. The symptoms of the cancer, the side effects of treatment or both can make it very difficult to achieve adequate intake. Using extra fats and carbohydrates is the easiest way to increase calories. If possible, choose the better fats and the better carbohydrates. If and when it becomes too much of a struggle to eat enough or drink enough then using any kind of fat or carbohydrate is okay. What might limit your choices is the type of side effects you are experiencing or if you are following a special diet for other conditions. For instance, if you are a person with diabetes it is not a good idea to introduce high-sugar foods. If you fall into this category, it is best to speak with your dietitian about what to do.

AVERAGE DAY	HIGH-PROTEIN, HIGH-CALORIE DAY
Breakfast	**Breakfast**
1/2 cup cereal	1/2 cup cereal
	with 1/2 tbsp raisins and 1/2 tbsp almonds
1/2 cup skim milk	1/2 cup 2% milk
1 slice toast	1 slice toast
1 tsp jam	with 1 tbsp peanut butter and 1 tsp jam
tea	tea
Lunch	**Lunch**
1 cup tossed salad	1 cup tossed salad
1 tbsp salad dressing	1 tbsp salad dressing
	with 1 chopped hard-cooked egg
small dinner roll	small dinner roll
	with 1 pat butter
1 cup water	1/2 cup water
	mixed with 1/2 cup juice
Afternoon Snack	**Afternoon Snack**
1 medium pear	1 medium pear
Dinner	**Dinner**
4 oz baked chicken breast	4 oz baked chicken breast
1/2 cup mashed potatoes	1/2 cup mashed potatoes
	with 1 pat butter
1/2 cup carrots	1/2 cup carrots
	drizzled with 1/2 tbsp olive oil
1/2 cup juice	1/2 cup 2% milk
Evening Snack	**Evening Snack**
1/2 cup JELL-O®	1/2 cup pudding
Total Protein = 55 grams	Total Protein = 80 grams
	An extra 25 grams
Total Calories = 1000	Total Calories = 1600
	An extra 600

Sample Menu

This sample menu is intended to increase protein and calories. It may not represent a well balanced diet.

Breakfast
Mini Pancakes*
Fruit topped with cream
Small glass of homogenized milk

Morning Snack
Date, Raisin and Nut Muffin*
Small glass of juice

Lunch
Tuna Melt*
Vegetables and Dip*
Small glass of homogenized milk

Afternoon Snack
Easy Baked Custard*

Dinner
Spanish Rice with Meatballs*
Small salad with olive oil and vinegar
Small glass of juice

Evening Snack
Roll-up*
Herb Scone*
Small drink

* Recipes are from Chapter 1 – *Loss of Appetite.*

Recipe Index

CROSSOVER RECIPES

Peanut Butter Banana Smoothie

Who doesn't like peanut butter and banana? A smoothie differs from a milkshake in its lack of ice cream.

1/2 cup	unflavoured soy beverage, milk or high-protein milk	125 mL
1	ripe banana, cut into chunks	1
2 tbsp	smooth peanut butter	25 mL
1 tbsp	honey, or to taste	15 mL

In blender, purée all ingredients until smooth.

Makes a 1-cup (250 mL) serving.

Per serving: cal 400, pro 13 g, fat 19 g, carb 53 g, fibre 4 g

Tips
- Soy beverages are particularly appropriate for those who are lactose-intolerant.
- Pour over ice, if desired.
- To make high-protein milk, pour 2 cups (500 mL) of homogenized milk into a bottle or a jar with a lid. Add 1/2 cup (125 mL) skim milk powder, screw on lid and shake until milk powder dissolves. Refrigerate before using.

Tasty Tidbit
Did you know that soy products do not naturally contain calcium? Many companies have added calcium to their soy beverages, so look for this on the label.

DIPS FOR VEGETABLES

Baby carrots that come prewashed are an incredible convenience. Pieces of celery, peppers and mushrooms work well with these dips too. So do crackers and pita wedges.

SPINACH DIP

1	package (10 oz/300 g) frozen spinach	1
1/2 cup	sour cream or plain yogurt	125 mL
1/2 cup	mayonnaise	125 mL
3	green onions, thinly sliced	3
1	clove garlic, chopped	1

Cook spinach on stovetop or in microwave, according to package directions. Rinse under cold water. Drain well and squeeze dry. Chop coarsely.

In blender or food processor, purée spinach, sour cream, mayonnaise, green onions and garlic until smooth. Refrigerate at least 1 hour. May be stored in refrigerator for 4 days.

Makes about 1 1/2 cups (375 mL).

Per serving (2 tbsp/25 mL): cal 89, pro 1 g, fat 9 g, carb 2 g, fibre 1 g

TASTY TIDBIT
All dark green, leafy vegetables provide vitamin A, but did you know that spinach is also a good source of lutein? This nutrient is showing great promise in the area of eye health.

Bean Dip

Use with canned navy or white lima beans. Add a 170 g can chunk or flaked tuna, drained, to this dip to make it even heartier.

1	can (19 oz/540 mL) white beans, drained and rinsed	1
1/3 cup	mayonnaise	75 mL
1	clove garlic, chopped	1
	salt to taste	
1/2 tsp	pepper	2 mL
1 tbsp	lemon juice	15 mL

In blender or food processor, process beans, mayonnaise, garlic, salt, pepper and lemon juice until smooth. Refrigerate at least 1 hour before serving. May be stored in refrigerator for 4 days.

Makes 1 3/4 cups (425 mL).

Per serving (2 tbsp/25 mL): cal 76, pro 2 g, fat 4 g, carb 7 g, fibre 2 g

Nachos

You can also add sliced green or black olives.

1/2	bag (330 g) tortilla chips	0.5
1/2 cup	prepared salsa	125 mL
1 cup	shredded Cheddar and mozzarella cheeses	250 mL

Arrange tortilla chips evenly on an ungreased pizza pan or shallow baking sheet. Spoon salsa over top. Sprinkle with cheeses.

Place about 6 inches (15 cm) under broiler for 3 to 5 minutes, or just until cheeses melt.

Makes 4 servings.

Per serving: cal 314, pro 10 g, fat 19 g, carb 28 g, fibre 3 g

Tip

• To make 1 serving, arrange 2 large handfuls of tortilla chips on a microwavable dinner plate. Spoon 2 tbsp (25 mL) salsa on chips, then sprinkle with 1/3 cup (75 mL) shredded cheese. Microwave on medium until cheese melts, about 1 minute.

Tasty Tidbit

Did you know that cooked tomato products, including salsa, are a good source of lycopene? This antioxidant is also found in watermelon and pink grapefruit.

Edamame

Edamame are fresh soybeans in pods. They are smaller than lima beans and have a sweet nutty taste and crunchy texture. Serve warm or cold as a snack. Add to salads, pasta dishes, stir-frys or as an interesting garnish to soup. Look for them in the frozen food section of the grocery store.

1	package (1 lb/500 g) frozen edamame	1

In large saucepan, bring 8 cups (2 L) water to a boil. Add frozen edamame and return to a boil. Cook for 5 to 8 minutes or until tender. Drain and rinse with cold water. Shell beans from pods and discard pods.

Makes 6 servings.

Per serving: cal 53, pro 5 g, fat 2 g, carb 4 g, fibre 2 g

Tasty Tidbit
Did you know that this green soybean originated in China, where it was called *mao dou*? It picked up the popular name edamame when it was introduced in Japan.

Roll-Ups

Substitute any deli meat for the turkey. For a heartier variation, place a slice of Cheddar cheese between the turkey and pear slices.

2	large, round, thick-cut deli turkey slices	2
2 tsp	honey mustard	10 mL
2 tsp	mayonnaise	10 mL
1	ripe but firm pear, cut into 8 to 10 thin slices	1

Place turkey slices on a work surface. Combine honey mustard and mayonnaise. Carefully spread mixture on each turkey slice. Arrange pear slices on top of each turkey slice. Roll up and wrap in plastic wrap. Refrigerate for 2 to 4 hours.

To serve, cut each roll in half.

Makes 2 servings.

Per serving: cal 139, pro 6 g, fat 6 g, carb 17 g, fibre 3 g

Tasty Tidbit
Do you avoid buying pears because they are too hard? Put them in a paper bag on the counter and they will continue to ripen.

Mini Frittatas

2/3 cup	combined diced red and green pepper	150 mL
10	eggs	10
2 tbsp	milk or cream	25 mL
1/2 tsp	salt	2 mL
1/4 tsp	pepper	1 mL
1/2 cup	shredded Cheddar or mozzarella cheese	125 mL

Divide red and green peppers among 12 cups of a well greased muffin pan. Place in preheated 375°F (190°C) oven and cook for 8 minutes to soften the peppers.

In bowl, whisk eggs, milk, salt and pepper. Pour evenly over peppers in cups, filling only 2/3 full (mixture will puff up during baking). Sprinkle cheese over each.

Return to 375°F (190°C) oven and bake 12 to 15 minutes or until eggs are set. Serve warm.

Makes 12 small frittatas, 4 to 6 servings.

Per serving: cal 249, pro 19 g, fat 17 g, carb 3 g, fibre 0 g

Tips
- If desired, add 2/3 cup (150 mL) of chopped cooked vegetables or ham to egg mixture instead of the peppers.
- Recipe may be halved.
- Cooked frittatas can be frozen in small freezer bags for a convenient snack. To reheat from frozen, bake for 20 minutes in preheated 375°F (190°C) oven.
- If you do not have a muffin pan, use a well greased 9-inch (23 cm) pie plate and increase baking time of egg mixture 20 to 25 minutes or until set.

Tasty Tidbit
Did you know that red and green peppers come from the same plant? Red peppers are green peppers that have been allowed to ripen further.

Mini Pancakes

If desired add 1/4 cup (50 mL) chocolate chips, chopped dried apricots or blueberries to batter. Serve with your favourite syrup. For extra calories, top pancakes with butter or margarine.

1/2 cup	buttermilk	125 mL
1/2 cup	plain yogurt	125 mL
1	egg	1
1/2 tsp	vanilla	2 mL
1 cup	all-purpose flour	250 mL
1 1/2 tsp	baking powder	7 mL
1/4 tsp	salt	1 mL
	butter (for cooking)	

In large measuring cup or bowl, whisk together buttermilk, yogurt, egg and vanilla.

In another bowl, stir together flour, baking powder and salt. Gradually whisk dry ingredients into buttermilk mixture just until blended. Batter will be thick.

Heat a large skillet over medium heat. Melt about 1 tbsp (15 mL) butter in skillet. Pour about 2 tbsp (25 mL) batter into skillet to form a small pancake. Repeat until skillet is full. Cook for 1 to 3 minutes or until bubbles appear on top and underside is golden brown. Carefully flip with a spatula and cook for an additional 30 to 60 seconds or until underside is golden brown. Repeat with remaining batter, adding butter as needed.

Makes about 15 mini pancakes, 4 to 5 servings.

Per serving: cal 153, pro 6 g, fat 4 g, carb 23 g, fibre 1 g

Tips
- One tbsp (15 mL) each of lemon juice and lemon zest makes a lovely addition to batter.
- Reheat any leftover pancakes in a toaster oven or microwave oven.

Tasty Tidbit
Did you know that you can purchase eggs that contain omega-3 fatty acids? Using these eggs can add a healthy fat to your recipes.

Monte Cristo Sandwich

The Monte Cristo sandwich is a grilled cheese sandwich that has been "French-toasted."

2	slices whole-wheat bread	2
1	slice (1 oz/30 g) Cheddar cheese	1
1	egg	1
1 tsp	milk	5 mL
	salt and pepper to taste	
1 tsp	butter or margarine	5 mL

Make a sandwich of bread and cheese slice. In a shallow bowl, beat together egg, milk, salt and pepper. Dip both sides of sandwich in egg mixture until fully coated.

Heat a small skillet over medium heat. Melt butter and cook sandwich about 3 minutes per side or until sandwich is golden brown on both sides.

Makes 1 serving.

Per serving: cal 377, pro 20 g, fat 21 g, carb 29 g, fibre 4 g

Tip
• Spread some mustard on cheese slices before topping with second bread slice or add a slice of ham to sandwich.

Tasty Tidbit
Not all whole-grain breads have the same amount of fibre or the same number of calories. A slice of whole-wheat bread may actually have more fibre and fewer calories than a slice of 7-Grain bread. Read the labels – it is surprising what you can learn.

Tuna Melts

Substitute 2 hard-cooked eggs for the tuna and make egg salad.

1	can (170 g) flaked or chunk tuna, drained	1
2 tbsp	mayonnaise	25 mL
1 1/2 tsp	pickle relish or chopped green onion	7 mL
few drops	lemon juice	few drops
2	English muffins, halved	2
1/4 cup	shredded cheese	50 mL

In bowl, combine tuna, mayonnaise, relish or green onion and lemon juice. Divide tuna mixture among muffin halves. Sprinkle with cheese and broil until cheese melts.

Makes 2 servings.

Per serving: cal 365, pro 23 g, fat 17 g, carb 28 g, fibre 2 g

Tip
• Add a slice of tomato or avocado under the cheese.

Tasty Tidbit
Did you know that canned tuna is a good source of omega-3 fatty acids? These healthy fats are also found in other fatty fish, like salmon and herring, and in flax seed, black walnuts and wheat germ.

So Simple Cheesy Pizza

An English muffin or a small flour tortilla can be used in place of the pita, see tips below.

1	Greek style whole-wheat pita	1
1/4 cup	prepared pizza or spaghetti sauce	50 mL
3/4 cup	shredded mozzarella cheese	175 mL

Place pita on a baking sheet. Spread sauce over top and sprinkle with cheese.

Bake in preheated 450°F (230°C) oven for 10 minutes or until cheese melts. Let stand 2 minutes before cutting and eating.

Makes 1 serving.

Per serving: cal 459, pro 24 g, fat 23 g, carb 41g, fibre 6 g

Tips
- Add 1/4 cup (50 mL) thinly sliced vegetables – try mushrooms, peppers or onion.
- For variety, use a different shredded cheese such as a four-cheese blend or crumbled feta cheese.
- If using an English muffin or a 6-inch (15 cm) tortilla, reduce pizza sauce to 3 tbsp (45 mL), cheese to 1/3 cup (75 mL) and cooking time to 7 to 8 minutes.

Tasty Tidbit
If you want a vegetarian treat, use soy cheese instead of regular cheese and a plain tomato purée instead of sauce.

Mushroom Tortilla Pizza

1	6-inch (15 cm) flour tortilla	1
1/4 cup	prepared mild salsa or pizza sauce	50 mL
1/4 cup	sliced mushrooms	50 mL
1/4 cup	shredded mozzarella or Cheddar cheese	50 mL

Place tortilla on baking sheet. Spread salsa evenly over tortilla leaving 1/4-inch (1 cm) bare around edges (sauce will spread during cooking). Top with mushrooms and sprinkle with cheese.

Bake in preheated 450°F (230°C) oven for 10 minutes or until cheese melts.

Makes 1 serving.

Per serving: cal 203, pro 9 g, fat 9 g, carb 22 g, fibre 2 g

Tips

- If desired, substitute 1/4 cup (50 mL) chopped peppers or cooked spinach for the mushrooms. Sauté the vegetables in a little butter or vegetable oil to make them even tastier.
- OLÉ: For a Mexican variation, spread 2 tbsp (25 mL) refried beans evenly over tortilla, then top with salsa, mushrooms and cheese and bake as above.

Tasty Tidbit

Are you always using white button mushrooms in recipes? Try experimenting with a variety of mushrooms to discover rich flavours and meaty textures. Tantalize your taste buds with Shiitake or Portobello varieties in sauces and stir-frys.

Mushroon Tortilla Pizza

Meat and Potato Pizza

Here is a chunky, meaty pizza with a crisp crust.

1	6-inch (15 cm) flour tortilla	1
1/4 cup	prepared salsa or pizza sauce	50 mL
1/4 cup	diced cooked potato	50 mL
1/2 cup	diced cooked chicken, turkey, beef or sausage	125 mL
1/4 cup	shredded mozzarella or Cheddar cheese	50 mL

Place tortilla on baking sheet. Spread salsa or pizza sauce evenly over tortilla. Top with potatoes and meat. Sprinkle cheese over top.

Bake in preheated 450°F (230°C) oven for 8 to 10 minutes or until cheese begins to bubble around the edges. Let stand 2 minutes before cutting and eating.

Makes 1 serving.

Per serving: cal 364, pro 30 g, fat 14 g, carb 29 g, fibre 3 g

Tasty Tidbit

How can you boost the fibre content of a traditionally low-fibre dish? Look for ways to add whole grains. For example, whole-wheat tortillas are available in most stores and they can be substituted for regular tortillas.

Peanut Butter Crispy Squares, p.43

Stuffed Baked Potato

Potatoes are an easy way to get potassium and vitamin C into your diet. Top with 1 to 2 tbsp (15 to 25 mL) of any of the topping suggestions.

1	medium or large potato	1
Toppings:	salsa	
	shredded cheese	
	sautéed onions, mushrooms or zucchini	
	chopped broccoli and shredded Cheddar cheese	
	cottage cheese	
	sour cream or yogurt	

Scrub potato and pierce with fork. Place directly on oven rack and bake in preheated 425°F (225°C) oven for 1 hour or until potato is tender. Cut a cross in potato and top with desired topping.

Makes 1 serving.

Per potato (with broccoli and cheese): cal 281, pro 9 g, fat 5 g, carb 52 g, fibre 5 g

Tips

• For a crispier skin, lightly rub potato with vegetable oil before baking.

• *To cook a potato in a microwave*: Scrub and pierce potato in several places. Place on paper towel and microwave 1 potato 3 to 6 minutes on high, depending on size, until tender. Turn over partway through cooking. Let stand a few minutes before cutting.

• *How to pick a potato*: There are many varieties of potatoes, but they are generally classified as long, round whites and round reds. Long potatoes are sometimes labelled Russets or baking potatoes and tend to have dark, thick skins and a dry, fluffy texture – good for baking, mashing and frying. Round whites and round reds can range in size from small to quite large and are firm-fleshed, higher in water and lower in starch than long whites. These hold their shape during cooking, making them ideal for potato salads, scalloped potatoes, boiling, steaming, sautéing or roasting. Yukon Gold potatoes are a yellow-fleshed all-purpose potato, suitable for baking, roasting or mashing.

Tasty Tidbit

Do you know how cottage cheese got its name? It was originally made in European cottages with the milk left over from making butter.

Simple Skillet Supper

Serve with rice, pasta or potatoes, as desired.

4	boneless skinless chicken breasts	4
1/2 tsp	dried thyme, oregano or Italian seasoning	2 mL
1/2 tsp	salt	2 mL
1/4 tsp	pepper	1 mL
3 tbsp	butter	45 mL
4	green onions, chopped	4
1/4 lb	mushrooms, sliced	125 g
1 tsp	sugar	5 mL
1 tsp	salt	5 mL
2 tbsp	lemon juice	25 mL
1/2 cup	apple juice	125 mL
2	tomatoes, diced	2
3 tbsp	chopped fresh parsley	45 mL

Season chicken with thyme, salt and pepper.

In large skillet, melt butter over medium heat and lightly brown chicken on both sides.

Add mushrooms around chicken and sauté for 1 to 2 minutes. Add remaining ingredients except parsley and stir lightly to mix.

Cover and cook on low heat for 25 to 30 minutes or until chicken is tender. Sprinkle with parsley.

Makes 4 servings.

Per serving: cal 279, pro 34 g, fat 11 g, carb 11 g, fibre 2 g

Tip
• Chopped green or red pepper can also be added with the mushrooms.

Tasty Tidbit
Did you know that the white meat of chicken is easier to digest than the dark meat? It has a little less connective tissue and a little less fat.

Mini Burgers

Once cooked, cool and freeze the burgers separately for a quick meal. Reheat in oven or in microwave. Serve in small round rolls.

1 lb	ground beef, veal, chicken or turkey	500 g
1/4 cup	corn flake or dry bread crumbs	50 mL
1 tbsp	ketchup	15 mL
1	clove garlic, minced or 1 tsp (5 mL) bottled garlic	1
1 tbsp	finely chopped onion	15 mL
1/4 tsp	each salt and pepper	1 mL

In bowl, lightly combine ground meat, crumbs, ketchup, garlic, onion, salt and pepper. Shape into 6 or 8 small patties, about 1/4-inch (5 mm) thick and 3 1/2 to 4 inches (10 cm) in diameter.

Place on a foil-lined shallow-rimmed baking sheet. Broil for about 5 minutes per side or until each side is browned.

Makes 6 to 8 burgers.

Per burger: cal 144, pro 14 g, fat 7 g, carb 4 g, fibre 0 g

Tip

• Reheat frozen burgers in microwave on medium for 1 1/2 to 2 minutes each, or in preheated 350°F (180°C) oven for 10 minutes.

Tasty Tidbit

Do you have trouble with burgers falling apart while cooking? You can solve the problem by refrigerating the formed patties for about half an hour before cooking.

Easy Beef Satays

Use small skewers for appetizers and longer ones for a main course. Pork strips, cut from a boneless pork sirloin steak or a leg inside or outside steak can be used in place of beef.

1 lb	sirloin, sirloin tip or round steak	500 g
1/2 cup	teriyaki sauce	125 mL
1 tsp	grated fresh ginger	5 mL
1	clove garlic, minced	1
	fresh coriander leaves, optional	
	peanut sauce	

Cut beef into long strips, about 1/2-inch (1 cm) wide.

In medium bowl, combine teriyaki sauce, ginger and garlic. Add beef strips and stir to coat. Let stand at room temperature for 15 minutes or cover and refrigerate several hours.

If using wooden skewers, soak skewers in cold water about 15 minutes before use to prevent charring during cooking.

Remove meat from marinade and weave strips loosely on skewers. Broil or grill about 4 minutes, turn over and cook a few more minutes until tender and only slightly pink inside. Garnish with coriander, if using and serve with peanut sauce.

Makes 4 servings.

Per serving: cal 131, pro 19 g, fat 4 g, carb 3 g, fibre 0 g

Tasty Tidbit
It is important for food safety to discard any marinade if raw meat, poultry or fish has been in it. If you need to moisten food near the end of cooking, make some fresh marinade for basting.

Spanish Rice with Meatballs

This quick 'n easy one-skillet supper serves up comfort food when you don't feel like fussing.

1 lb	lean ground beef	500 g
1	clove garlic, minced	1
1/2 tsp	dried oregano	2 mL
2 tbsp	vegetable oil	25 mL
1/2 cup	sliced mushrooms	125 mL
1	medium zucchini, sliced	1
1 3/4 cups	pasta sauce with vegetables	425 mL
1 1/2 cups	water	375 mL
1 1/2 cups	instant white rice	375 mL
1/2 cup	grated Parmesan or Romano cheese	125 mL

Combine beef, garlic and oregano; with moist hands shape into 1-inch (2.5 cm) meatballs.

In large skillet, heat oil over medium heat. Add meatballs and cook until evenly browned.

Push meatballs to sides of pan, add mushrooms and zucchini and stir-fry for 2 minutes.

Combine pasta sauce and water; stir into meatballs and vegetables. Bring to a boil, then stir in rice. Cover and simmer 5 minutes.

Remove from heat and stir. Cover and let stand 5 minutes. Sprinkle each serving with cheese.

Makes 4 servings.

Per serving: cal 561, pro 32 g, fat 29 g, carb 41g, fibre 4 g

Tips
- If desired, substitute ground chicken or turkey for ground beef.
- Diced onion, about 1/4 cup (50 mL), can be added with mushrooms and zucchini.
- Alternatively, meatballs can be baked in a preheated 350°F (180°C) oven for 10 to 12 minutes.

Tasty Tidbit
If you feel up to it, cook some extra meatballs and store in the freezer. Take them out and add to soups and sauces for some extra protein or enjoy a couple as a tasty snack.

Simple Sautéed Fish Fillets

1/4 cup	all-purpose flour	50 mL
1/2 tsp	salt	2 mL
1/2 tsp	dried herbs – basil, dill, thyme, oregano or tarragon leaves	2 mL
	pepper to taste	
1 lb	sole, tilapia, haddock, catfish or other white fish fillets, in 4 portions	500 g
1 tbsp	vegetable oil	15 mL
	lemon wedges	
	melted butter	

Combine flour, salt, herbs and pepper in shallow dish. Thoroughly dredge fish fillets in flour mixture (discard any leftover mixture).

Heat oil in large skillet over medium-high heat. Add fish, working in batches, if necessary, and cook until lightly browned and fish is tender, about 3 to 4 minutes per side. Serve with lemon wedges and/or drizzle with a little melted butter.

Makes 4 servings.

Per serving: cal 143, pro 20 g, fat 5 g, carb 5 g, fibre 0 g

Tasty Tidbit

If using frozen fish, check packages for signs of thawing and refreezing. Frozen fish should be solidly frozen, have a mild aroma and be free of ice crystals and freezer burn.

Scones with Herbs

2 cups	all-purpose flour	500 mL
2 tbsp	granulated sugar	25 mL
1 tbsp	baking powder	15 mL
1/3 cup	finely chopped parsley	75 mL
1 tsp	dried thyme leaves	5 mL
1/2 tsp	salt	2 mL
1/4 tsp	dried rosemary	1 mL
1/2 cup	cold butter, cubed	125 mL
1	egg	1
2/3 cup	milk or high-protein milk	150 mL

In large bowl, combine flour, sugar, baking powder, parsley, thyme, salt and rosemary. Using two knives or pastry blender, cut in butter until mixture is crumbly.

In small bowl, lightly beat egg; add milk. Add this mixture all at once to dry ingredients, stirring with a fork to make a light, soft dough. Gather into a ball and turn out onto a lightly floured surface.

With floured hands, knead gently a few times until smooth. Roll or pat dough out to a 3/4-inch (2 cm) thickness. Using a 2 1/2-inch (7 cm) floured cutter, cut out rounds. Place on ungreased baking sheet. Gather up scraps and repat dough; cut out more rounds. Brush tops with milk.

Bake in preheated 425°F (220°C) oven for 12 to 14 minutes or until golden. Let cool on wire racks.

Makes 12 scones.

Per scone: cal 167, pro 3 g, fat 9 g, carb 19 g, fibre 1 g

Tip
• To make high-protein milk, pour 2 cups (500 mL) of homogenized milk into a bottle or a jar with a lid. Add 1/2 cup (125 mL) skim milk powder, screw on lid and shake until milk powder dissolves. Refrigerate before using.

Tasty Tidbit
Store dry herbs carefully to lock in flavour. Keep them in a tightly covered container in a cool, dry and dark place.

EASY BAKED CUSTARD

4	eggs	4
3/4 cup	granulated sugar	175 mL
2 1/2 cups	milk, high-protein milk or cream	625 mL
1 tsp	vanilla	5 mL

In large bowl whisk together eggs, sugar, milk and vanilla until thoroughly combined. Pour into six 6-oz (175 mL) ramekins or custard cups.

Place ramekins in a 13- x 9-inch (3.5 L) baking pan. Pour enough hot water into pan to come halfway up ramekins. Bake in preheated 350°F (180°C) oven for 50 to 60 minutes or until knife inserted in centres comes out creamy. Remove from water and cool on wire rack. Serve warm or refrigerate up to 3 hours to serve chilled.

Makes 6 servings.

Per serving: cal 198, pro 7 g, fat 5 g, carb 30 g, fibre 0 g

TIP
- To make high-protein milk, pour 2 cups (500 mL) of homogenized milk into a bottle or a jar with a lid. Add 1/2 cup (125 mL) skim milk powder, screw on lid and shake until milk powder dissolves. Refrigerate before using.

TASTY TIDBIT
Do you know why custard cups are placed in water for baking? The water prevents the custard from heating too quickly and cracking.

Black and White Ice Cream Sandwiches

If desired, substitute with favourite ice cream or frozen yogurt.

6	chocolate wafers	6
3 tbsp	vanilla ice cream, softened	45 mL

Scoop or spoon about 1 tbsp (15 mL) of ice cream on 3 wafers. Top with remaining wafers. Freeze sandwiches on a baking sheet until solid, then wrap individually and place in freezer bag. Return to freezer and use within 1 month.

Makes 3 servings.

Per serving: cal 69, pro 1 g, fat 3 g, carb 11 g, fibre 0 g

Tasty Tidbit
For some extra fun, drizzle caramel sauce over ice cream before topping with the remaining wafers.

Peanut Butter Crispy Squares

A treat the whole family will enjoy.

1/2 cup	semi-sweet chocolate chips	125 mL
1/2 cup	brown sugar	125 mL
1/2 cup	peanut butter	125 mL
1/2 cup	corn syrup	125 mL
1 tbsp	butter	15 mL
3 cups	crispy rice cereal	750 mL

In large microwavable bowl, combine chocolate chips, sugar, peanut butter, corn syrup and butter. Microwave uncovered on high for 2 to 3 minutes or until mixture melts. Stir partway through cooking.

Stir in cereal with a wooden spoon until well blended. Press evenly into a lightly buttered 8-inch square (2 L) baking dish.

Refrigerate until firm, about 1 hour. Cut into squares.

Makes 16 squares.

Per square: cal 154, pro 3 g, fat 6 g, carb 24 g, fibre 1 g

Tasty Tidbit

If you have a peanut allergy, you can substitute almond butter. This will still provide a good source of protein and great flavour.

Peanut Butter Cookies

1 1/2 cups	all-purpose flour	375 mL
1/4 tsp	baking soda	1 mL
1/4 tsp	baking powder	1 mL
1/8 tsp	salt	0.5 mL
1/2 cup	butter, softened	125 mL
1/2 cup	peanut butter, smooth or crunchy	125 mL
1/2 cup	granulated sugar	125 mL
1/4 cup	brown sugar	50 mL
1	egg	1
1/2 tsp	vanilla	2 mL
1/2 cup	chocolate chips (optional)	125 mL

In bowl, combine flour, baking soda, baking powder and salt. Set aside.

In large bowl using an electric mixer, beat butter, peanut butter, and sugars together until light and fluffy. Beat in egg and vanilla until smooth. Gradually beat in dry ingredients on medium-low speed until blended. Stir in chips, if using.

Shape dough into 1-inch (2.5 cm) balls. Place about 2 inches (5 cm) apart, on parchment paper or greased cookie sheets. With a floured fork, press down each cookie to 1/2-inch (1 cm) thickness.

Bake in preheated 350°F (180°C) oven for 10 to 12 minutes, or until lightly browned. Cool on wire rack.

Makes 2 dozen cookies.

Per cookie: cal 139, pro 3 g, fat 8 g, carb 16 g, fibre 1 g

Tip
• If dough if too soft to shape into balls, chill dough for about 1 hour for easier handling.

Tasty Tidbit
Peanut butter cookies are an excellent travelling treat if you know you will be at the hospital for most of the day. Pair them up with milk (the cookie's best friend), and you have a nutritious snack.

DATE, RAISIN AND NUT MUFFINS

Once cooled, pop into a freezer bag for later use.

1 1/2 cups	all-purpose flour	375 mL
1/3 cup	brown sugar	75 mL
1 1/2 tsp	baking powder	7 mL
1/2 tsp	baking soda	2 mL
1/4 tsp	each, nutmeg and salt	1 mL
1/2 cup	chopped dates	125 mL
2 tbsp	raisins	25 mL
2 tbsp	chopped pecans	25 mL
2	eggs	2
1/3 cup	vegetable oil	75 mL
1/2 tsp	vanilla	2 mL
1 cup	milk or high-protein milk	250 mL

In large bowl, combine flour, brown sugar, baking powder, baking soda, nutmeg and salt. Toss dates, raisins and pecans in flour mixture to prevent sticking together.

In smaller bowl, whisk eggs, oil, vanilla and milk together. Stir into dry ingredients just until blended.

Spoon or pour batter into well greased muffin cups. Bake in preheated 400°F (200°C) oven for 18 to 20 minutes, or until toothpick inserted in centre comes out clean. Let cool in pan on wire rack for 5 minutes. Transfer to rack to cool completely.

Makes 12 muffins.

Per muffin: cal 191, pro 4 g, fat 8 g, carb 26 g, fibre 1 g

TIP
- To make high-protein milk, pour 2 cups (500 mL) of homogenized milk into a bottle or a jar with a lid. Add 1/2 cup (125 mL) skim milk powder, screw on lid and shake until milk powder dissolves. Refrigerate before using.

TASTY TIDBIT
Did you know that most of the fat in pecans is monounsaturated fat? This type of fat is good for heart health – in moderation, of course!

Trail Mix

If desired, substitute cashews or pecans for the peanuts.

1 tbsp	butter	15 mL
1 1/2 cups	shelled, salted peanuts	375 mL
1/2 cup	shelled sunflower seeds	125 mL
1 1/2 cups	raisins	375 mL
1 cup	shredded coconut	250 mL
1/2 cup	dried banana chips	125 mL
1/3 cup	chopped dried apricots	75 mL

In large skillet, melt butter over medium heat. Add peanuts and sunflower seeds stirring until lightly browned, about 3 minutes.

Transfer to large serving bowl. Stir in remaining ingredients one at a time and toss to mix thoroughly. Store in tightly covered container.

Makes 6 cups (1.5 L).

Per serving (1/4 cup/50 mL): cal 139, pro 4 g, fat 8 g, carb 15 g, fibre 2 g

Tasty Tidbit

Did you know that sunflower seeds have a greater amount of vitamin E per ounce than any nuts or other seeds? Other good sources are nuts, especially almonds and hazelnuts, oils, peanut butter and cooked spinach.

CHAPTER 2

Dealing *with* Nausea

Introduction

Nausea can occur for many different reasons. Some chemotherapy drugs, as well as certain medications, such as those for pain, can cause nausea to develop. Nausea may also be caused by radiation therapy to the abdomen and pelvic area, throat, upper chest or brain.

The recipes in this chapter are designed to help you deal with nausea. They focus on more easily tolerated foods. These foods are usually bland, low in odour, and lower in fat and fibre.

Getting enough fluids is important to prevent dehydration, so many of these recipes contain liquids as their main ingredient. Some people find that eating and drinking at the same time makes them feel more nauseated. If this bothers you, separate your liquids and solids at meals.

HELPFUL HINTS FOR YOU

- Eat small meals frequently throughout the day. Nausea can be worse when your stomach is empty.
- Use dry, starchy foods such as crackers and toast to help settle your stomach.
- Choose foods that are cold or room temperature. They tend to have less odour than hot foods.
- Remain in an upright position for an hour after eating. Lying down right after eating can make nausea worse.
- Sip fluids throughout the day to help maintain your hydration.
- Drink through a straw if you are sensitive to smells.
- Avoid your favourite foods when you are nauseated to help prevent a permanent dislike for that food.
- Avoid wearing tight clothing around the waist. This is a good time for sweat pants with an elasticized waist.
- Try sipping on peppermint tea or sucking on a peppermint candy, as this may help ease nausea.

HELPFUL HINTS FOR THE CAREGIVER

- Offer small amounts of food and beverages often.
- Allow your loved one to say "no" to food occasionally. During periods of severe nausea, it is more important that they sip fluids regularly.
- Try to keep track of how much fluid they are drinking in a day. Consult a doctor if it is low for more than 1 day, especially if they are also vomiting.
- Cook when your loved one is not home, so they are not exposed to cooking aromas. If this is not possible, make sure they are not in the kitchen, and open windows while cooking.
- If friends are asking what they can do, let them help by cooking something at their homes.
- Take out the kitchen garbage on a regular basis. Food odours from garbage can make nausea worse.

How to Modify a Meal Plan

AVERAGE DAY	DAY WHEN FEELING NAUSEATED
	7 am 2 soda crackers
Breakfast – 8 am 2 eggs on buttered toast 3/4 cup orange juice 1 cup coffee	**Breakfast – 8 am** 1 dry toast 1/2 banana 3/4 cup tea
10 am 1 cup coffee	**10 am** 3/4 cup flat ginger ale
	11 am 3/4 cup JELL-O®
Lunch – 12 pm 1 cup cream of mushroom soup tuna sandwich with mayo apple 1 cup 2% milk	**Lunch – 12 pm** 3/4 cup chicken noodle soup 1/2 cheese sandwich
2 pm 1 cup tea 1 donut	**2 pm** 3/4 cup tea 2 ginger cookies
	4 pm 3/4 cup diluted juice
Dinner – 6 pm 1/4 chicken large serving scalloped potatoes broccoli tomato and cucumber salad 1 cup water	**Dinner – 6 pm** 1 slice of chicken without skin 1/2 cup mashed potato made with broth 1/2 cup melon
	7 pm 3/4 cup diluted nectar
8 pm 1 cup hot chocolate 1 butter tart	**8 pm** 3/4 cup flat ginger ale 2 social tea cookies
	9 pm 3/4 cup water

Sample Menu

This sample menu is intended to increase fluids to promote good hydration. It does not represent a well balanced diet.

Breakfast
Fruit Cream of Wheat®*
Tea

Morning Snack
Frozen Jelly Pop*
Flat ginger ale

Lunch
Turkey slices on white bread
Vegetable Broth*
Lemon Syrup Drink*

Afternoon Snack
Easy Sugar Cookies*
Berry Ice*

Dinner
Pasta noodles lightly sprinkled with grated mozzarella cheese
(Use a pat of butter on pasta to help moisten cheese.)
Applesauce Jelly*

Evening Snack
Angel food cake
Mint Orange Iced Tea*

* Recipes are from Chapter 2 – *Dealing with Nausea.*

Recipe Index

CROSSOVER RECIPES

Lemon Syrup

This concentrated syrup is great for a quick and refreshing glass of lemonade.
Simply stir 2 tbsp (25 mL) syrup with 3/4 cup (175 mL) cold water. For a
soothing hot drink, mix 2 tbsp (25 mL) syrup with 3/4 cup (175 mL) boiling
water. This syrup also makes a tasty addition to iced tea.

1 1/2 cups	granulated sugar	375 mL
1/2 cup	boiling water	125 mL
1 1/2 cups	freshly squeezed lemon juice	375 mL
	(3 medium lemons)	

In heatproof bowl, stir boiling water and sugar until sugar dissolves. Stir in lemon
juice. Cover and refrigerate. Use within 3 days.

Makes 2 cups (500 mL).

Per serving (2 tbsp/25 mL): cal 78, pro 0 g, fat 0 g, carb 21 g, fibre 0 g

Tip
• To get more juice out of lemons, microwave each lemon for 20 seconds. Alternately,
  roll lemons on counter top a few times before squeezing.

Tasty Tidbit
For some variety of flavour, orange and lime syrups can also be made, just by
substituting orange or lime juice for the lemon juice in the recipe.

Ginger Syrup

Pour this syrup over yogurt, cottage cheese or sliced bananas. Or use to flavour applesauce or rice pudding, or to make a soothing tea.

1 cup	sliced fresh ginger, about 4 knobs, unpeeled	250 mL
1 1/2 cups	water	375 mL
1 cup	granulated sugar	250 mL

In small saucepan, bring water, sugar and ginger to a boil over medium heat, stirring to dissolve sugar. Remove from heat and let stand for 15 to 20 minutes.

Pour syrup through a sieve and discard ginger. Cover and refrigerate. Use within 3 days.

To freeze syrup, pour into ice cube trays. Cover and freeze. Use within 1 month.

Makes 1 1/2 cups (375 mL).

Per serving (2 tbsp/25 mL): cal 65, pro 0 g, fat 0 g, carb 17 g, fibre 0 g

Ginger Tea

Stir 2 tbsp (25 mL) ginger syrup into 1 cup (250 ml) hot water.

Per serving: cal 65, pro 0 g, fat 0 g, carb 17 g, fibre 0 g

Tasty Tidbit
The strong flavour of ginger can help ease symptoms of nausea. Sip on flat ginger ale or nibble on ginger cookies to help settle your stomach.

Mint Orange Iced Tea

Keep this tea in a large pitcher in the refrigerator and drink as desired.

1/2 cup	water	125 mL
1 cup	granulated sugar	250 mL
1/2 cup	fresh mint leaves, chopped	125 mL
4 cups	freshly brewed tea	1 L
2 cups	orange juice	500 mL

In small saucepan, stir water and sugar together. Bring to a boil over medium heat; add mint leaves and simmer 2 minutes. Remove from heat and stir to blend. Cool to room temperature. When cool, strain and reserve mint syrup, discard mint leaves.

Make tea by steeping 4 tea bags in 4 cups (1 L) of boiling water in teapot or heatproof bowl for 4 minutes.

In large pitcher, combine tea, orange juice and mint syrup. Cover and refrigerate. Use within 3 days.

Makes 6 cups (1.5 L).

Per serving (1 cup/250 mL): cal 168, pro 1 g, fat 0 g, carb 43 g, fibre 0 g

Tasty Tidbit

The refreshing taste of mint may help settle an upset stomach. It might be helpful to take a few mint candies with you when you are away from home.

Green Tea Citrus Punch

A punch of vitamin C and antioxidants is a bonus to this refreshing tea mixture that can be sipped all day long. The health benefits of green tea are varied and well established.

2 cups	boiling water	500 mL
2	green tea bags	2
1/2 cup	honey	125 mL
1 cup	orange juice	250 mL
1/2 cup	freshly squeezed lemon juice (2 lemons)	125 mL
2 cups	ginger ale	500 mL

In heatproof bowl, pour boiling water over tea bags. Let steep 4 minutes. Remove bags and discard.

Stir in honey, orange and lemon juices and ginger ale.

Cover and refrigerate. Use within 3 days.

Makes about 6 cups (1.5 L).

Per serving (1 cup/250 mL): cal 136, pro 0 g, fat 0 g, carb 36 g, fibre 0 g

Tasty Tidbit

Did you know that green tea and black tea come from the same plant? The tea leaves are processed differently to produce the different varieties.

GINGER LEMONADE

Soothing and refreshing.

1 tbsp	minced fresh ginger	15 mL
4 cups	water	1 L
1/2 cup	freshly squeezed lemon juice (about 2 lemons)	125 mL
1/2 cup	granulated sugar or honey	125 mL

In saucepan, combine ginger and water and bring to a boil.

Add lemon juice. Reduce heat and simmer for 15 minutes.

Stir in sugar until dissolved. Remove from heat and cool to room temperature.

When cooled, cover and refrigerate. Use within 3 days.

Makes about 4 cups (1 L).

Per serving (1 cup/250 mL): cal 105, pro 0 g, fat 0 g, carb 28 g, fibre 0 g

TASTY TIDBIT
Ginger is a knobby, fibrous root, with a smooth light brown skin, available in most supermarkets. Look for ginger root with the least amount of knots and/or branching, and store it in a cool, dry place. Ginger can also be peeled and kept in the freezer.

Fruit Cream of Wheat®

The fruit you can add to this is limitless; use seasonal fresh fruit, or canned or thawed frozen fruit out of season.

2 cups	milk	500 mL
2 tbsp	granulated sugar	25 mL
1/2 tsp	salt	2 mL
1/4 cup	quick (not instant) Cream of Wheat® cereal	50 mL
3/4 cup	chopped fresh or canned fruit or frozen fruit, thawed	175 mL

In small saucepan, bring milk, sugar and salt to a simmer over medium-high heat. Slowly pour in Cream of Wheat® and cook until thickened, 1 to 2 minutes, stirring constantly.

Remove from heat and stir in fruit. Serve warm.

Makes about 2 1/2 cups (625 mL).

Per serving (1/2 cup/125 mL): cal 111, pro 4 g, fat 2 g, carb 19 g, fibre 1 g

Tasty Tidbit

Did you know that Cream of Wheat® is a good source of iron? The vitamin C in fruit helps your body absorb iron better.

Apricot Honey Oatmeal

If you like, add some raisins to this oatmeal.

3	finely chopped dried apricots	3
pinch	cinnamon	pinch
1	package instant plain oatmeal	1
3/4 cup	boiling water	175 mL
2 tsp	honey	10 mL

Put apricots, cinnamon and oats in a bowl. Add boiling water and stir until oats are thoroughly moistened. Add honey and serve.

Makes 1 serving.

Per serving: cal 226, pro 5 g, fat 2 g, carb 49 g, fibre 4 g

Tasty Tidbit

Did you know that dried apricots are a good source of vitamin A and potassium? They travel well and make an easy take-along snack.

Vegetable Broth

Clear broth served lukewarm or at room temperature can help to relieve nausea. Other vegetables, such as potatoes, and mushrooms can be added to this simplified version of vegetable stock. Freeze portions individually to be used when desired. Add some steamed white rice to soup if desired.

10 cups	water	2.5 L
1	medium onion, quartered	1
4	carrots, cut in 2-inch (10 cm) chunks	4
4	stalks celery, cut into 2-inch (10 cm) chunks	4
1 cup	fresh parsley sprigs	250 mL
1 1/2 tsp	salt	7 mL

In large soup pot or saucepan, combine water, onion, carrots, celery, parsley and salt. Bring to a boil, reduce heat and simmer 1 to 2 hours.

Strain soup through a large sieve or colander into a large container. Cool broth to room temperature. Divide into individual portions, refrigerate or freeze.

Makes 8 cups (2 L).

Per serving (1 cup/250 mL): cal 23, pro 0 g, fat 0 g, carb 5 g, fibre 0 g

Tips
- For an Asian twist, add some fresh grated ginger to vegetable mixture when making broth. Ginger is especially beneficial in helping to reduce nausea. Flavour with soy sauce after cooking.
- For soup, add cooked rice or small pasta or thin egg noodles.
- For vegetable soup, add chopped carrots, potatoes, peas, or any favourite vegetables, and cook until vegetables are tender. You can also add tomato paste, and fresh or dried herbs after cooking as desired.

Tasty Tidbit
Drinking clear broth can help to keep you hydrated throughout the day. It may be a nice change from sweet drinks.

Broth-Based Soup Ideas

Ever increasing ranges of broth — vegetable, chicken and beef — are available making it simple to make a nourishing bowl of soup. Tetra Pak broths are particularly convenient; just use straight from the carton. Canned broths generally require diluting with an equal amount of water. Dry cube or sachet broths are reconstituted with boiling water. Just be aware that many of these can be quite salty.

Stracciatella Soup (Version 1)

1	egg	1
1 tsp	minced parsley	5 mL
	salt and pepper to taste	
1 cup	broth	250 mL

In small bowl, beat egg with parsley, salt and pepper. Set aside.

In small saucepan, bring broth to a boil.

Slowly pour egg mixture into boiling broth and gently stir so that egg mixture breaks up into pieces.

Once egg mixture is completely cooked, remove from heat.

Makes about 1 1/2 cups (375 mL).

Per serving (3/4 cup/175 mL): cal 48, pro 3 g, fat 3 g, carb 0 g, fibre 0 g

Tips
- Try these tasty variations:
  - Add small size pasta such as pastina or orzo to simmering broth. Cook until pasta is tender.
  - Add cooked plain white rice to simmering broth.
  - *Egg-Drop Soup*: Add 1/2 tsp (2 mL) minced fresh ginger and 1 sliced green onion to broth and bring to a boil. Add egg as above, and season with a few drops of soy sauce, if desired.

Tasty Tidbit
Stracciatella means "little rags or shreds." This is due to the thread-like look of the egg once it is stirred into the soup. This Italian egg-drop soup makes a wonderful comfort food.

Pear Ginger Sorbet

Ginger has been found to ease nausea. Pears and ginger come together in a very easy-to-make, refreshing and delicious sorbet. If desired, serve with a drizzle of warm chocolate sauce. Easy and refreshing!

1	can (14 oz/398 mL) pears in light syrup	1
1 tsp	fresh peeled ginger, minced	5 mL

Place pears, syrup and ginger in blender and blend until smooth. Pour into small bowl and freeze until firm, about 2 hours. To serve, scoop into serving dishes. Use within 3 days.

Makes 3 servings.

Per serving: cal 70, pro 0 g, fat 0 g, carb 18 g, fibre 2 g

Tasty Tidbit

Pears are a close cousin of the apple, and are a good source of fibre. The spiciness of ginger is offset by the sweetness of the pear, resulting in a fantastic combination of flavours!

Berry Ice

Cold foods that are soft in texture and sweet in taste are easily tolerated. Take the berries out of the freezer 20 minutes before making the ice.

2 cups	frozen unsweetened berries	500 mL
1 1/2 cups	water	375 mL
1/2 cup	honey	125 mL
2 tbsp	lemon juice	25 mL

In blender or food processor, purée berries, water, honey and lemon juice until smooth. Pour into plastic or glass bowl or container and freeze for 6 hours or until firm.

Remove from freezer about 15 minutes before serving. Scoop with an ice cream scoop. Use within 5 days.

Makes about 4 cups (1 L).

Per serving (1/2 cup/125 mL): cal 84, pro 0 g, fat 0 g, carb 23 g, fibre 1 g

Tip
• Fruit Ice: Try with any frozen fruit such as sliced peaches or mangoes.

Tasty Tidbit
Frozen mixed berries are available all year round. They can be thawed and added to cereal or used as a topping for yogurt or ice cream. If your mouth is sore, frozen blueberries are a softer choice.

Vanilla Cupcakes, p.70

PEACH SHERBET

Make this and freeze in individual portions to take out as desired.

2 cups	frozen unsweetened peach slices, chopped	500 mL
1/2 cup	plain, vanilla or peach yogurt	125 mL
2 tbsp	orange juice	25 mL
3 tbsp	granulated sugar	45 mL

In blender or food processor, purée peaches, yogurt, juice and sugar until smooth.

Pour mixture into individual freezer-safe containers and freeze until firm, about 1 hour. Use within 3 days.

Makes about 2 1/2 cups (625 mL).

Per serving (1/2 cup/125 mL): cal 77, pro 2 g, fat 0 g, carb 17 g, fibre 1 g

Tip
• This can be made with other frozen fruit, even fresh or canned as long as they are frozen before going into the food processor. Keep a stock of berries (strawberries, raspberries, blueberries) or a berry blend in the freezer. If using fresh or canned fruit, drain canned fruit well, chop and freeze until solid.

Tasty Tidbit
Sherbet is refreshing, and is not as heavy as ice cream. This makes it easier to tolerate when you are not feeling well.

Hoisin and Orange Glazed Chicken, p.89

Frozen Jelly Pops

If you don't have frozen pop moulds, small paper cups work well. Choose compatible flavours of jelly and drink mix.

1	package (85 g) jelly powder	1
1	package (6 g) powdered unsweetened drink mix	1
1/2 cup	granulated sugar	125 mL
2 cups	boiling water	500 mL
2 cups	cold water	500 mL

In heatproof bowl, pour boiling water over jelly powder, drink mix and sugar. Stir until dissolved.

Stir in cold water. Pour into frozen pop moulds or 3-oz (85 mL) waxed paper cups. Freeze partially, about 1 1/2 to 2 hours. Push clean craft sticks into centre of each. Freeze until firm, another 3 to 4 hours. To serve, peel paper off pop.

Makes 12 to 14 pops.

Per pop: cal 59, pro 1 g, fat 0 g, carb 15 g, fibre 0 g

Frozen Pudding on a Stick

Push a clean flat craft stick through centre of foil cover on a snack-size pudding cup. Freeze upright for 2 hours or until firm. To serve, remove foil cover from around stick. Dip plastic cup in very hot tap water for one minute, then squeeze the plastic cup to release the pudding. If too firm, allow pudding pop to sit in a small dish in the refrigerator until desired consistency. Once frozen, the pudding cups can be stored in a plastic bag in the freezer until needed.

Per serving: cal 147, pro 3 g, fat 4 g, carb 25 g, fibre 0 g

Tasty Tidbit

Did you know that popsicles were invented in 1905 by an 11-year-old named Frank W. Epperson? First called "Epsicles," these frozen treats were accidentally created when Frank left his glass of lemonade on the back porch overnight with the stirring stick still in it.

Applesauce Jelly

Two easily blended foods are also easily combined. Try your favourite jelly flavour.

1	package (85 g) jelly powder mix	1
1 cup	boiling water	250 mL
1 1/2 cups	unsweetened applesauce	375 mL

In heatproof bowl, stir boiling water into jelly powder until dissolved. Blend in applesauce until smooth.

Divide mixture into 6 serving dishes. Cover and refrigerate until firm, 2 to 3 hours.

Makes 3 cups (750 mL).

Per serving (1/2 cup/125 mL): cal 80, pro 1 g, fat 0 g, carb 20 g, fibre 1 g

Tips

Easy Apple Ideas in the microwave:

• For a quick single serving of applesauce, peel, core and chop 1 apple into a small microwavable bowl. Add 1 tbsp (15 mL) water. Cover and microwave on high for 2 to 3 minutes or until tender. Stir well and add sugar to taste. Makes 1/2 cup (125 mL).

• *Baked Apple Halves*: Cut 1 apple in half through the stem. Use a melon baller or spoon to remove core and stem. Pierce skin in several placing to prevent skin from bursting during cooking. Place halves, cut side up in a shallow microwavable dish. Sprinkle each half with 1 tsp (5 mL) brown sugar and a pinch of cinnamon or nutmeg. Microwave, uncovered on high for 1 to 2 minutes or until apple is tender. Makes 2 servings.

Tasty Tidbit

Did you know that the Northern Spy apple is the variety of apple with the highest level of antioxidants? This makes them a good choice for applesauce.

Cool 'n' Fruity Dessert Cups

A quick, refreshing dessert. Try different flavours of jelly powder with different canned fruits.

1	can (14 oz/398 mL) peach and pear chunks in juice	1
1	package (85g) strawberry jelly powder	1
1 cup	boiling water	250 mL
2 cups	ice cubes	500 mL

Drain fruit. Divide fruit among four dessert dishes.

In heatproof bowl, pour boiling water over jelly powder. Stir until completely dissolved. Add ice cubes, stirring until mixture begins to thicken.

Remove unmelted ice with a slotted spoon. Pour mixture slowly over fruit in dishes. Chill until set, 15 to 20 minutes.

Makes 4 servings.

Per serving: cal 110, pro 2 g, fat 0 g, carb 27 g, fibre 1 g

Tasty Tidbit

Canned fruit has been heated – basically cooked in the can – so it is much softer than raw fruit. This makes it a good choice if your mouth is sore.

Tea Biscuits

Biscuits are popular for the speed in which they can be made. A light hand in kneading gives the treasured flaky result. Baked biscuits can be frozen individually.

2 cups	all-purpose flour	500 mL
1 1/2 tsp	baking powder	7 mL
1 tsp	salt	5 mL
1/2 cup	cold butter, cubed	125 mL
3/4 cup	milk	175 mL

In large bowl, combine flour, baking powder and salt. Using two knives or pastry blender, cut in butter until mixture is crumbly. Pour milk over top and stir with fork until a soft, slightly sticky dough is formed.

Place dough on lightly floured surface. With floured hands, knead gently about 10 times. Roll or pat dough out to a 1/2-inch (1 cm) thickness. Using a 2-inch (5 cm) floured cutter, cut out rounds. Place on ungreased baking sheet. Gather up scraps and repat dough; cut out more rounds. Brush tops with milk or melted butter.

Bake in preheated 400°F (200°C) oven for 12 to 15 minutes or until golden. Let cool on wire racks.

Makes 12 biscuits.

Per biscuit: cal 160, pro 3 g, fat 9 g, carb 17 g, fibre 1 g

Tip

- Biscuit flavours are easily varied, if desired. Dust them, before baking with cinnamon and sugar. Or incorporate into the dough, any of the following:
  - 2 tbsp (25 mL) finely chopped fresh herbs (parsley, chives, dill or sage)
  - 1/2 cup (125 mL) shredded Cheddar cheese
  - 1/2 cup (125 mL) raisins or currants

Tasty Tidbit

These simple biscuits can be eaten anytime, and you may feel better with a small amount of solid food in your stomach. Nibbling dry or starchy foods can be helpful in relieving symptoms of nausea.

Vanilla Cupcakes

Once baked and cooled, cupcakes can be easily frozen (without icing) for a later use.

1 1/2 cups	all-purpose flour	375 mL
1 tsp	baking powder	5 mL
1/4 tsp	salt	1 mL
1/2 cup	butter or margarine, softened	125 mL
3/4 cup	granulated sugar	175 mL
3	eggs	3
2 tsp	vanilla	10 mL
1/2 cup	milk, lukewarm	125 mL

Lightly grease muffin cups or line with fluted paper baking cups.

In a bowl, stir together flour, baking powder and salt. Set aside.

In another bowl, beat butter and sugar with an electric mixer on high until light and fluffy. Reduce speed to medium and beat in eggs and vanilla. On low speed, add dry ingredients alternately with milk just until blended.

Spoon batter into prepared muffin cups until 3/4 full. Bake in preheated 350°F (180°C) oven for 20 to 22 minutes, until cake tester inserted in centre comes out clean. Let cool in pan on rack for 5 minutes. Transfer to rack to cool completely.

Makes 12 cupcakes.

Per cupcake: cal 199, pro 4 g, fat 9 g, carb 25 g, fibre 0 g

Tips
- For easier portioning into muffin cups, use a spring-loaded ice cream scoop.
- Additions, if desired:
  - Stir 1/2 cup (125 mL) chocolate chips or chopped chocolate into dough.
  - Dust before baking, with cinnamon or sugar.
  - Dust after baking, with sifted icing sugar or cocoa.
  - Cupcakes may be left plain, or spread with a thin layer of icing.

Tasty Tidbit
Did you know that the vanilla plant is a member of the orchid family? The extract is expensive because the vanilla flowers have to be hand-pollinated, and the pods have to be cured for months!

Lemon Loaf

Once baked and cooled, slices of lemon loaf can be easily frozen for a later use.

1 1/2 cups	all-purpose flour	375 mL
1 tsp	baking powder	5 mL
1/4 tsp	salt	1 mL
1 tbsp	finely grated lemon peel	15 mL
1/2 cup	butter or margarine, softened	125 mL
3/4 cup	granulated sugar	175 mL
2	eggs	2
1/2 tsp	vanilla	2 mL
1/2 cup	milk	125 mL

Grease an 8- x 4-inch (1.5 L) loaf pan.

In a bowl, stir together flour, baking powder, salt and lemon peel. Set aside.

In another bowl, beat butter and sugar with an electric mixer on high until light and fluffy. Reduce speed to medium and beat in eggs, one at a time until smooth. Add vanilla. On low speed, add dry ingredients alternately with milk just until blended.

Spread batter into prepared pan. Bake in preheated 350°F (180°C) oven for 50 to 55 minutes, until cake tester inserted in centre comes out clean. Let cool in pan on rack for 5 minutes. Transfer to rack to cool completely.

Makes 1 loaf, 12 slices.

Per slice: cal 192, pro 3 g, fat 9 g, carb 25 g, fibre 1 g

Tips
- To make lemon cupcakes, divide batter into muffin cups and bake in preheated 350°F (180°C) oven for 20 to 22 minutes, or until cake tester inserted in centre comes out clean.
- For easier portioning into muffin cups, use a spring-loaded ice cream scoop.

Tasty Tidbit
Slices of this simple cake are great straight from the toaster, topped with jam. Try a slice with some Mint Orange Iced Tea (page 56).

Plain Muffins

These muffins are as basic as you can get. If desired, add 1/2 cup (125 mL) of any of the following: chocolate chips, fresh or frozen blueberries, raisins, dried cranberries or mashed ripe banana.

1 1/2 cups	all-purpose flour	375 mL
1/4 cup	granulated sugar	50 mL
2 tsp	baking powder	10 mL
1/2 tsp	salt	2 mL
3/4 cup	milk, lukewarm	175 mL
2	eggs	2
1/4 cup	melted butter or margarine	50 mL

Grease muffin pan or line with fluted paper baking cups.

In large bowl, combine flour, sugar, baking powder and salt.

In another bowl, whisk together milk, eggs and butter. Pour over dry ingredients and stir with a wooden spoon just until dry ingredients are mixed. Spoon into prepared pan, about 2/3 full.

Bake in preheated 400°F (200°C) for 16 to 20 minutes or until tops are firm to the touch. Let cool in pan on rack for 5 minutes. Transfer to rack to cool completely.

Makes 12 muffins.

Per muffin: cal 128, pro 3 g, fat 5 g, carb 17 g, fibre 0 g

Tips
- Muffin batters are easily made. To mix, add the beaten liquid ingredients to dry ingredients; stir lightly, only until combined (ignore the lumps). If the batter is stirred longer, the gluten in the flour will develop and toughen the dough.
- For ease, use a spring-loaded ice cream scoop to portion dough into muffin cups.
- For savoury muffins, reduce sugar to 1 tbsp (15 mL) and add 1/2 cup (125 mL) shredded Cheddar cheese to flour mixture. If desired, sprinkle tops with additional cheese.

Tasty Tidbit
Did you know that the name "muffin" might come from the French word "moufflet," meaning soft bread, or from the German word "muffe" which is the name for a type of cake?

Ways with Angel Food Cake

Angel Food Cake is always a favourite and is easy to dress up. Prepared cakes are readily available in traditional size (about 8 servings) and mini Angel cakes, (6 to a package). If you like to bake, an Angel Food Cake mix can be made in either a large tube pan; two 9- x 5-inch (2 L) loaf pans; one 13- x 9-inch (3.5 L); or in two 12-cup muffins pans to make cupcakes. Just follow package directions.

Here are some suggestions to quickly jazz up Angel Food Cake:
- Top with fresh fruit such as sliced strawberries, blueberries, bananas, mangoes or peaches.
- Top with drained canned fruit such as peaches, fruit cocktail, or pears.
- Top or fill cake with prepared pie filling such as cherry, blueberry, apple or lemon. Make up a Lemon Pie Filling mix and cool. Slice Angel Food Cake in half horizontally; spread bottom half with about 1 cup (250 mL) lemon filling. Place top half of cake on filling. Mix remaining lemon filling with about 2 cups (500 mL) thawed whipped dessert topping and use to frost cake.
- Top with applesauce or apricot or peach baby food.
- Garnish with a dollop of whipped cream, or dessert topping.
- Serve with a scoop of vanilla ice cream, sherbet or frozen yogurt.
- Serve with pudding (homemade or prepared), vanilla custard, flavoured yogurt or ricotta cheese.
- Cut into cubes and skewer on bamboo stick together with fruit such as strawberries, grapes and bananas to make dessert kabobs.
- Use to make mini trifles.

Pineapple Cloud Cake

Made with only two ingredients, this produces a light dessert. Serve with a dollop of whipped cream, if desired. Prepare one Angel Food Cake mix according to package directions, adding one 14-oz (398 mL) can crushed pineapple (juice included). Spread in greased 13- x 9-inch (3.5 L) baking pan. Bake in preheated 350°F (180°C) oven for 30 to 40 minutes or until top is brown, firm and feel dry. Cool completely on wire rack and serve from pan.

Makes 15 servings.

Per serving: cal 120, pro 3 g, fat 0 g, carb 28 g, fibre 0 g

Tasty Tidbit
Angel Food Cake likely originated with the Pennsylvania Dutch, who developed the cake mould required for this cake. It is a yeast-free cake that uses many egg whites. It is thought that this cake came about as a use for leftover egg whites.

Easy Sugar Cookies

If desired, sprinkle tops with a little granulated sugar before baking. One or two of these makes a satisfying snack.

1 1/4 cups	all-purpose flour	300 mL
1/2 tsp	baking soda	2 mL
3/4 cup	granulated sugar	175 mL
1/2 cup	soft margarine	125 mL
1/2 tsp	vanilla	2 mL
1	egg white	1

In small bowl, combine flour and baking soda. In large bowl, whisk together margarine and sugar until light and creamy. Whisk in vanilla and egg white. Stir in flour mixture until combined.

Shape into a log, about 2 inches (5 cm) in diameter. Wrap in plastic wrap and refrigerate for a few hours or until firm.

Cut into 1/4-inch (5 mm) thick slices. Place about 2 inches (5 cm) apart on parchment paper-lined or lightly greased cookie sheet.

Bake in preheated 375°F (190°C) oven for 7 to 8 minutes or until lightly golden.

Transfer to wire rack to cool completely.

Makes 2 dozen cookies.

Per cookie: cal 83, pro 1 g, fat 4 g, carb 11 g, fibre 0 g

Tasty Tidbit

Eating small amounts of food regularly throughout the day can help settle symptoms of nausea. These plain cookies are easy to digest and a handy snack to have around.

CHAPTER 3

Taste *Changes*

Introduction

The recipes in this chapter are suitable for people who are experiencing taste changes during cancer treatment. You may have a bitter or metallic taste in your mouth or you may find that food has absolutely no flavour at all. Your taste sensations may also change from day to day. Everyone is affected differently.

Radiation to the head and throat, some chemotherapy drugs, antibiotics, painkillers and other drugs can all affect taste. These changes may persist for a while after your treatment has finished. Don't be concerned as it may take some time before your ability to taste returns. Just keep experimenting – what is unpleasant today may become appealing again tomorrow.

HELPFUL HINTS FOR YOU

- Try cold or room temperature drinks. They may be better tolerated than hot beverages. For example: mint- or lemon-flavoured water and fruit smoothies are better tolerated than hot coffees. Crushing mint leaves releases more flavour.

- Season food with different herbs and sauces to enhance the food's flavour. For example: onion, garlic, ketchup, or mint.

- Keep tart foods and fluids handy. Orange, lime or lemon juice can help cover a metallic taste.

- Experiment with sugar and salt. A sprinkle of sugar can tone down a salty or bitter taste and a dash of salt can tone down an overly sweet or acidic taste.

- Use ketchup, salsa or hot sauces to add a flavour boost to bland foods such as eggs.

- If you find that meat has a bitter and metallic taste, try other high protein foods such as poultry, dairy foods, peanut butter, eggs, tofu, fish, and legumes.

- Add horseradish or mustard to sandwiches and other foods.

- Try fruit sorbet, sherbet and fruit smoothies for a refreshing drink (recipes found in Chapter 2 – *Dealing with Nausea).*

- If you also have a sore mouth, do not use spicy or acidic foods and drinks.

HELPFUL HINTS FOR THE CAREGIVER

- If your loved one is experiencing a metallic taste to foods, use glass pots for cooking and have plastic utensils on hand. This can lessen the metallic taste.

- Don't hesitate to use more herbs and spices in your cooking. The extra flavour will be appreciated.

- Make popsicles using their favourite juice. This will also help with improving fluid intake.

- If you find yourself running out of time, make food preparation easier by preparing things ahead. Spaghetti sauce can be made in large batches that can be frozen in individual meal portions and thawed to make a quick meal at a later date.

- There are no rules as to when certain foods need to be eaten. If breakfast foods are well tolerated, prepare those foods for dinner.

- If your loved one has a sore mouth, do not use spicy or acidic foods and drinks.

How to Modify a Meal Plan

AVERAGE DAY	DAY WITH ADDED FLAVOUR
Breakfast	**Breakfast**
plain bagel	cinnamon bagel
with plain cream cheese	with peanut butter
apple juice	mango peach juice
coffee	coffee
sugar	sugar
2% milk	2% milk
Lunch	**Lunch**
roast beef sandwich	egg salad sandwich
	with pickles
vanilla pudding	fruit yogurt
banana	tangerine
water	lemonade
Afternoon Snack	**Afternoon Snack**
vanilla milkshake	fruit smoothie
Dinner	**Dinner**
4 oz steak	4 oz orange glazed chicken breast
mashed potatoes	fried rice
boiled carrots and peas	grilled vegetables
	drizzled with balsamic vinegar
plain yogurt	strawberry ice cream
apple juice	iced tea
Evening Snack	**Evening Snack**
custard	fruit sorbet

Sample Menu

This sample menu is intended to improve and enhance the taste of food. It may not represent a well balanced diet.

Breakfast
Creamy Maple Oatmeal**
Toast and peanut butter
Milk
Juice

Lunch
Gazpacho Soup* with crackers
Egg salad sandwich
Orange, Avocado and Mango Salad*
Lemon-flavoured water

Afternoon Snack
Yogurt

Dinner
Juice
Halibut with Mustard Sauce*
Roasted Rosemary Potatoes*
Peas with seasoned butter and sliced almonds
Fresh or canned peach halves
Milk

Evening Snack
Roasted Chickpeas*
Mint-flavoured water

* Recipes are from Chapter 3 – *Taste Changes*.
** Recipes are from Chapter 4 – *Sore Mouth and Swallowing Problems*.

Recipe Index

CROSSOVER RECIPES

GUACAMOLE

Serve with pita or tortilla chips.

2	ripe avocados, halved, pitted and peeled	2
2 tbsp	lime or lemon juice	25 mL
2 tbsp	prepared salsa	25 mL
2 tbsp	minced onion	25 mL
1 tbsp	chopped fresh cilantro or parsley	15 mL
2 tsp	minced fresh garlic	10 mL
1/4 tsp	chili powder	1 mL

In bowl, mash avocados and lime juice with a fork. Stir in salsa, onion, cilantro, garlic and chili powder.

Makes about 1 1/2 cups (375 mL).

Per serving (1/4 cup/50 mL): cal 108, pro 1 g, fat 10 g, carb 5 g, fibre 0 g

TIP
• If making ahead, cover with a thin layer of mayonnaise to prevent darkening.

TASTY TIDBIT
To pick a ripe avocado, choose one that gives way to your touch but isn't mushy. Avocados ripen 7 to 10 days after picking so if you want to slow the ripening process put it in the refrigerator. Otherwise, keep it on your kitchen counter.

Roasted Chickpeas

Great as a snack or added to salads. After cooling, these become quite crunchy.

1	can (19 oz/540 mL) chickpeas, drained and rinsed	1
2 tbsp	olive oil	25 mL
2 tsp	chili powder	10 mL
1/2 tsp	salt	2 mL

In large bowl, toss chickpeas with oil, chili powder and salt. Spread in 13- x 9-inch (3 L) baking pan.

Bake in preheated 400°F (200°C) oven for 60 to 70 minutes or until evenly browned, stirring or shaking pan every 15 minutes. Let cool completely. When cool store in airtight container at room temperature for up to 1 week.

Makes about 1 cup (250 mL).

Per serving (2 tbsp/25 mL): cal 104, pro 3 g, fat 4 g, carb 14 g, fibre 3 g

Tasty Tidbit
Chickpeas, also known as garbanzo beans, are members of the legume family. They are a good source of both protein and fibre.

Gazpacho

This soup is served cold. Substitute 1/2 cup (125 mL) chopped cucumber or celery for the yellow pepper, if desired.

2	large tomatoes, cored, seeded and finely chopped (about 2 cups/500 mL)	2
1	red pepper, seeded and finely chopped	1
1	yellow pepper, seeded and finely chopped	1
2 cups	plain yogurt	500 mL
1/2 cup	chopped fresh parsley	125 mL
1/2 cup	tomato juice	125 mL
6	green onions, thinly sliced (white parts only) or 1/3 cup (75 mL) finely chopped sweet onion	6
1/3 cup	red wine vinegar	75 mL
1/4 cup	olive oil	50 mL
2 - 3 tsp	minced fresh garlic	10 - 15 mL
1 tsp	salt	5 mL
1/2 tsp	pepper	2 mL

In a large bowl, stir together all ingredients. Serve at once or refrigerate, covered for up to 8 hours.

Makes 6 cups (1.5 L).

Per serving (1/2 cup/125 mL): cal 86, pro 3 g, fat 5 g, carb 7 g, fibre 1 g

Tip

- To seed tomatoes, cut in half crosswise. Cup one half in the palm of your hand and gently squeeze out seeds; repeat with remaining halves.

Tasty Tidbit

This refreshing cold soup is great on the go. The tomatoes are a great source of lycopene, an antioxidant that has been found to protect against prostate, lung and breast cancer as well as cardiovascular disease and certain eye diseases.

Easy Egg Salad

Serve as a sandwich filling on fresh multigrain bread or scoop on salad greens for a light lunch. For a snack, spread on crackers.

4	hard-cooked eggs, shelled and finely chopped	4
2 tbsp	mayonnaise	25 mL
2 tbsp	plain yogurt or sour cream	25 mL
1 tbsp	pickle relish	15 mL
1 tbsp	chopped onion	15 mL
1 tsp	curry powder	5 mL
1 tsp	paprika, optional	5 mL
1 tbsp	chopped fresh cilantro, optional salt and pepper	15 mL

In bowl, combine chopped eggs with mayonnaise, yogurt, relish, onion, curry powder and paprika and cilantro, if using. Add salt and pepper to taste.

Makes 1 1/4 cups (300 mL).

Per serving (1/4 cup/50 mL): cal 108, pro 5 g, fat 9 g, carb 2 g, fibre 0 g

Tips
- A pastry blender will chop eggs with little effort. For a finer texture, grate eggs on large holes of box grater.
- *For perfectly cooked eggs*: bring a saucepan of water to a boil. Gently place eggs in water and return to a boil. Simmer for 10 minutes. Drain and immediately place in cold water.

Tasty Tidbit
Cilantro is also known as Chinese parsley and is the same plant from which coriander seeds are harvested.

Couscous Salad

This is a versatile recipe. Instead of chickpeas, you can use kidney beans, steamed vegetables, olives, pine nuts, crumbled feta or goat cheese or a combination of ingredients.

Lemon Garlic Dressing:

1 tbsp	lemon juice	15 mL
1 tsp	minced fresh garlic	5 mL
1/4 tsp	ground cumin	1 mL
1/4 tsp	hot pepper sauce	1 mL
1/4 cup	olive oil	50 mL
	salt and pepper	

Salad:

1 1/4 cups	vegetable, beef or chicken broth	300 mL
1 cup	couscous	250 mL
1 cup	cooked chickpeas	250 mL

In bowl, combine lemon juice, garlic, cumin and hot pepper sauce. Gradually whisk in olive oil until blended. Season to taste with salt and pepper.

In saucepan or microwave, bring broth to a boil. Stir in couscous, remove from heat and let stand, covered, for 5 minutes or until tender. Fluff with a fork and transfer to a serving bowl. Add chickpeas and dressing, toss gently. Serve at room temperature.

Makes 4 servings.

Per serving: cal 370, pro 10 g, fat 15 g, carb 49 g, fibre 4 g

Tips

- You can use bottled minced garlic instead of chopped fresh garlic, or use 1/4 tsp (1 mL) garlic powder. Look for jars of garlic in the produce section.
- The dressing can also be used as a marinade for chicken, fish or tofu. Add 1 to 2 tbsp (15 to 25 mL) chopped fresh parsley for a kick of colour.

Tasty Tidbit

Couscous is made from durum wheat, the same wheat used to produce semolina pasta. It is widely available in supermarkets in the pasta/rice aisle.

Orange, Avocado and Mango Salad

This orange dressing is also good with a fresh fruit salad.

Dressing:

3/4 cup	orange juice	175 mL
2 tbsp	honey	25 mL
1 tbsp	olive oil	15 mL
1 tbsp	minced fresh ginger	15 mL

Salad:

5 cups	torn mixed salad greens	1.25 L
1	avocado, peeled, halved, pitted and thinly sliced	1
1	mango, peeled, halved and thinly sliced	1
2	large oranges, peeled and sectioned	2
1 cup	fresh raspberries or blueberries	250 mL

Dressing: In small bowl, whisk together orange juice, honey, oil and ginger.

In large bowl, toss greens lightly with some of the dressing (refrigerate any leftover dressing for another salad). Attractively arrange avocado, mango and orange slices on greens. Scatter berries on top.

Makes 4 servings.

Per serving (assuming all dressing is consumed):

cal 254, pro 3 g, fat 11 g, carb 40 g, fibre 4 g

Tasty Tidbit

Mangoes should be firm but give when pressed. If your mango is hard, place it on your counter in a paper bag with a piece of ripe fruit for a few days.

BBQ Chicken

Bottled barbecue sauce would work for this recipe, but this jazzed-up version improves it. Cut 2 or 3 large potatoes into wedges, toss with a little vegetable oil and a pinch of salt. Arrange on a lightly oiled baking sheet and bake along with chicken. Turn wedges over occasionally and bake until tender.

1/2 cup	prepared barbecue sauce	125 mL
1/4 cup	brown sugar	50 mL
2 tbsp	ketchup	25 mL
2 tbsp	water	25 mL
1 tbsp	lemon juice	15 mL
1 - 2 tsp	chili powder	5 - 10 mL
1/4 tsp	salt	1 mL
4	boneless, skinless chicken breasts	4

In bowl, whisk together barbecue sauce, brown sugar, ketchup, water, lemon juice, chili powder and salt.

Place chicken breasts in a lightly oiled or foil-lined rimmed baking sheet. Spoon sauce over chicken. Bake in preheated 350°F (180°C) oven for 30 to 40 minutes or until chicken is no longer pink inside.

Makes 4 servings.

Per serving: cal 275, pro 32 g, fat 2 g, carb 29 g, fibre 0 g

Tasty Tidbit

Chili powder is a combination of different types of dried chili peppers (most often ancho chili peppers), cumin and garlic powder. Different flavours are created by roasting the peppers or changing the varieties used.

Hoisin and Orange Glazed Chicken

Serve with rice and stir-fried vegetables.

1/2 cup	hoisin sauce	125 mL
1/4 cup	orange juice	50 mL
1 tbsp	soy sauce	15 mL
1 tbsp	grated fresh ginger	15 mL
8	skinless chicken pieces	8
	(thighs, breasts or legs)	

In bowl, combine hoisin sauce, orange juice, soy sauce and ginger.

Place chicken in lightly greased or foil-lined 13- x 9-inch (3 L) baking dish. Spoon sauce over chicken. Bake in preheated 375°F (190°C) oven for 30 to 40 minutes or until chicken is no longer pink in the centre.

Makes 6 to 8 servings.

Per serving (1 chicken piece): cal 113, pro 12 g, fat 3 g, carb 8 g, fibre 0 g

Tip
• You can use bottled minced ginger in place of fresh ginger, or use 1 tsp (5 mL) ground ginger. Look for jars of ginger in the produce section.

Tasty Tidbit
Chicken and turkey breasts should be checked for doneness using a meat thermometer. Insert the thermometer into the thickest part of the breast and when the thermometer reads 185°F (85°C) it is done.

Honey Mustard Chicken

Substitute turkey breasts or fish fillets for the chicken breasts, if desired.

2 tbsp	melted butter or margarine	25 mL
2 tbsp	honey	25 mL
1 tbsp	Dijon mustard	15 mL
1 tsp	curry powder	5 mL
1/2 tsp	salt	2 mL
4	boneless chicken breasts	4

In bowl, whisk together butter, honey, mustard, curry powder and salt.

Place chicken breasts in a lightly greased baking dish. Spoon sauce over chicken. Bake in preheated 350°F (180°C) oven for 30 to 35 minutes or until chicken is no longer pink in the centre. Spoon any juices left in pan over chicken when serving.

Makes 4 servings.

Per serving: cal 245, pro 33 g, fat 8 g, carb 9 g, fibre 0 g

Tasty Tidbit

Honey has a different flavour depending on what part of the country it comes from. Honey from Prince Edward Island has a pleasant flowery flavour because the bees are collecting pollen from wild flowers and blueberry bushes.

Lemon Chicken

Serve this chicken with steamed rice or a pilaf to absorb the lemon flavour.

1/3 cup	all-purpose flour	75 mL
1 tsp	paprika	5 mL
1/2 tsp	each, salt and pepper	2 mL
4	boneless chicken breasts	4
1 tbsp	olive oil	15 mL
1/2 cup	chicken broth	125 mL
2	lemons	2
2 tbsp	brown sugar	25 mL

In plastic bag, combine flour, paprika, salt and pepper. Shake chicken pieces in mixture until evenly coated.

In large skillet, heat oil over medium heat. Add chicken and cook for 2 minutes on each side or until lightly browned. Transfer to lightly greased 9-inch (2.5 L) square baking pan.

Grate rind from one lemon and squeeze juice. Mix broth, lemon rind and juice, and brown sugar together. Add to skillet and stir up any browned bits in pan. Pour over chicken in baking pan.

Slice second lemon into thin slices and arrange over chicken pieces. Bake in preheated 350°F (180°C) for 30 to 35 minutes or until chicken is no longer pink in centre.

Makes 4 servings.

Per serving: cal 241, pro 34 g, fat 6 g, carb 12 g, fibre 0 g

Tasty Tidbit

Paprika is made from mild peppers that have been dried and ground. Hungary and Spain are the two largest producers of this spice with the Hungarian variety being stronger and richer in flavour than the Spanish.

Savoury Chicken and Peaches

Serve this easy one-skillet supper with rice.

1 tbsp	vegetable oil	15 mL
4	skinless, boneless chicken breasts	4
1	small onion, chopped	1
1/2 cup	chopped green or red pepper (or mixed)	125 mL
2 tsp	medium curry powder, or to taste	10 mL
1	can (14 oz/398 mL) sliced peaches with juice	1
1/3 cup	mango chutney	75 mL
2 tsp	soy sauce	10 mL
	hot cooked rice	

In large skillet, heat oil over medium heat. Add chicken and cook until lightly browned on both sides.

Push chicken to sides of pan, sauté onion and peppers in centre of pan until tender, 1 to 2 minutes.

Stir in curry powder and cook briefly to develop flavour. Add peaches with juice, chutney and soy sauce. Stir ingredients together and simmer 1 to 2 minutes. Serve chicken, peaches and sauce with rice.

Makes 4 servings.

Per serving (rice not included): cal 319, pro 34 g, fat 6 g, carb 33 g, fibre 3 g

Tasty Tidbit
The mangoes, red peppers and peaches all add vitamin C to this savoury dish.

Halibut with Mustard Sauce

Serve with rice pilaf or boiled potatoes and a steamed green vegetable or salad. This could also be made with cod, salmon or red snapper fillets.

1 tbsp	granulated sugar	15 mL
1 tbsp	dry mustard	15 mL
1 tbsp	white vinegar	15 mL
1 tbsp	olive oil	15 mL
2	6-oz (175 g) halibut fillets	2
1/4 cup	fresh bread crumbs	50 mL

In bowl, whisk together sugar, mustard, vinegar and olive oil until sugar has dissolved and mixture is smooth. Line a small rimmed baking sheet with foil and grease foil well. Place fish, skin side down on foil. Brush fish with sauce. Press 2 tbsp (25 mL) fresh bread crumbs on top of mustard sauce on each piece of fish to form a crust.

Bake in preheated 450°F (230°C) oven for 10 to 14 minutes depending on thickness, until fish flakes easily with a fork.

Makes 2 servings.

Per serving: cal 253, pro 37 g, fat 8 g, carb 6 g, fibre 0 g

Variation
Replace sugar, vinegar and dry mustard with 2 tbsp (25 mL) Dijon mustard.

Tasty Tidbit
Fish such as halibut and salmon are good sources of omega-3 fatty acids that can help prevent heart disease.

Hoisin Salmon

Substitute haddock (a more economical option) or halibut for salmon.

2 tbsp	hoisin sauce	25 mL
1 tbsp	soy sauce	15 mL
1/4 tsp	pepper	1 mL
2	6-oz (175 g) salmon fillets	2
	(salmon wt includes skin)	

In bowl, whisk together hoisin sauce, soy sauce and pepper.

Line a small rimmed baking sheet with foil and grease foil well. Place fish, *skin side down* on foil. Brush fish with sauce. Marinate in refrigerator for 2 hours if time permits.

Bake in preheated 450°F (230°C) oven for 10 to 14 minutes depending on thickness, until fish flakes easily with a fork.

Makes 2 servings.

Per serving: cal 357, pro 35 g, fat 19 g, carb 8 g, fibre 0 g

Tasty Tidbit

Hoisin sauce, a Cantonese sweet bean sauce also known as *hoisin jiang*, is made of fermented soy beans, salt and garlic.

SWEET AND SOUR TOFU AND VEGETABLES

If you're in a hurry, substitute about 1/4 cup (50 mL) of a prepared sweet and sour sauce for this sauce. Serve with rice, if desired.

Sauce:

2 tbsp	orange juice	25 mL
2 tbsp	red wine vinegar	25 mL
1 1/2 tbsp	granulated sugar	22 mL
1 1/2 tsp	cornstarch	7 mL
1 1/2 tsp	soy sauce	7 mL
1/2 tsp	minced fresh garlic	2 mL
1/2 tsp	minced fresh ginger	2 mL
2 tbsp	vegetable or olive oil	25 mL
1 cup	sliced mushrooms	250 mL
1	red or green pepper, sliced	1
5	green onions, cut into 1-inch (2.5 cm) slices	5
1	package (350 g) firm or extra firm tofu, rinsed and cut into 3/4-inch (2 cm) cubes	1

In small saucepan, whisk together orange juice, vinegar, sugar, cornstarch, soy sauce, garlic and ginger. Bring to a boil over medium heat, whisking constantly. Cook until sauce thickens, about 3 minutes.

In large skillet, heat oil over medium-high heat. Add mushrooms, pepper, green onions and tofu and stir-fry for about 6 minutes or until vegetables are tender and tofu is browned. Add sauce, stir mixture to coat and serve immediately.

Makes 2 servings.

Per serving (without rice): cal 372, pro 17 g, fat 22 g, carb 32 g, fibre 4 g

TASTY TIDBIT

When purchasing tofu, look for brands that have been made with calcium sulphate. They are a good source of both protein and calcium.

Home Fries

This recipe makes good use of leftover potatoes. For an extra kick add a pinch of cayenne or hot pepper flakes.

2 tbsp	olive oil	25 mL
1	small onion, coarsely chopped or 6 sliced green onions	1
2	6 oz (175 g) baked or boiled potatoes (with or without skin), cut into 1/2-inch (1 cm) cubes	2
1 - 2 tsp	minced fresh garlic salt and pepper to taste	5 - 10 mL

In large nonstick skillet, heat oil over medium-high heat. Add onion and sauté until starting to soften but not brown. Add potatoes, garlic, salt and pepper and continue to sauté until potatoes are golden and heated through, 5 to 7 minutes.

Makes 2 servings.

Per serving: cal 264, pro 3 g, fat 14 g, carb 34 g, fibre 3 g

Tasty Tidbit

Instead of using Yukon Gold or regular potatoes try using purple or blue potatoes for a different colour. Potatoes also contain vitamin C that is most concentrated near the skin.

Individual Baked Alaskas, p.102

Roasted Rosemary Potatoes

For variety, substitute dill, parsley or tarragon for rosemary.

1 1/2 lbs	small new potatoes, scrubbed and unpeeled (18 to 20)	750 g
2 tbsp	olive oil	25 mL
1 tbsp	chopped fresh rosemary (or 1 tsp/5 mL dried)	15 mL
	salt and pepper to taste	

Toss potatoes with oil, rosemary, salt and pepper. Place in lightly greased 9-inch (2.5 L) square baking pan.

Bake in preheated 350°F (180°C) oven for 1 hour or until tender. Stir potatoes a few times during cooking.

Makes 4 servings.

Per serving (5 potatoes): cal 182, pro 3 g, fat 7 g, carb 28 g, fibre 2 g

Tasty Tidbit
New potatoes can be of any variety that is harvested early. The ones available in your supermarket are often the smaller red-skinned round potatoes which are in their prime late summer to early fall.

Banana Smoothie, p.110, Peach Smoothie, p.110, Vanilla Berry Smoothie, p.111

Sweet Potato Wedges

1	large sweet potato, peeled and cut into 6 to 8 wedges	1
2 tbsp	melted butter, margarine or olive oil	25 mL
	salt and pepper to taste	

Lightly oil a shallow baking pan or line with parchment paper or foil.

Toss wedges with butter, salt and pepper. Place wedges on pan and bake in preheated 425°F (220°C) oven for 15 to 20 minutes or until wedges are tender. Turn over halfway through cooking.

Makes 2 servings.

Per serving: cal 194, pro 2 g, fat 12 g, carb 22 g, fibre 3 g

Tips
- Try these tasty variations:
  - For added flavour, toss wedges with butter and 1 tsp (5 mL) grated orange rind, 1/4 tsp (1 mL) ground ginger and a pinch of cinnamon.
  - For a spicy version, use olive oil in place of butter and toss with 1/4 tsp (1 mL) each chili powder, cayenne and garlic powder.
- To make cutting easier, microwave sweet potato 1 to 2 minutes on high, then peel and cut into wedges.

Tasty Tidbit
To pick a sweet potato that packs the most vitamin A in it choose one that is deep orange in colour.

Mango Cranberry Sauce

Talk about versatile! This tart and tangy sauce can be used as a topping for yogurt or ice cream; an accompaniment for turkey, pork, chicken or fish; a dipping sauce; or spread over toast or English muffins.

1	bag (12 oz/340 g) fresh or frozen cranberries	1
2	mangoes, peeled and cut into chunks	2
1/2 cup	orange juice	125 mL
3/4 cup	granulated sugar	175 mL

In saucepan, combine cranberries, mangoes, orange juice and sugar. Bring to a boil and cook over medium heat until cranberries pop, stirring occasionally, about 10 minutes.

If making ahead, cool to room temperature, cover and refrigerate. Before serving, heat in microwave to room temperature. Store in refrigerator and use within 1 week or freeze for up to 3 months.

Makes 3 1/2 cups (875 mL).

Per serving (2 tbsp/25 mL): cal 38, pro 0 g, fat 0 g, carb 10 g, fibre 1 g

Tip
• Substitute 2 cups (500 mL) thawed, frozen mango for fresh mango.

Tasty Tidbit
Did you know that cranberries are indigenous to North America? They also have a naturally occurring chemical in them that aids in the treatment of urinary tract infections.

Mango Salsa

Serve with grilled or broiled fish, chicken, pork or tofu or as an appetizer with tortilla chips, pita crisps or crackers. For a little heat add a few dashes of hot pepper sauce.

1	mango, cut into 1/4-inch (5 mm) cubes	1
1	small tomato, seeded and diced	1
2	green onions, thinly sliced	2
2 tbsp	olive oil	25 mL
1 tbsp	minced fresh parsley or coriander leaves	15 mL
1 tbsp	chopped fresh mint	15 mL
1 tbsp	fresh lime juice	15 mL

In bowl, combine mango, tomato, onions, oil, parsley, mint and lime juice. It is best made at least 1 hour ahead for flavours to blend. Store in refrigerator for up to 3 days.

Makes 1 1/2 cups (375 mL).

Per serving (2 tbsp/25 mL): cal 34, pro 0 g, fat 2 g, carb 4 g, fibre 1 g

Tasty Tidbit

If you don't enjoy the fibrous texture of mangoes, try choosing a different variety of mango such as the Kent or Ataulfo. These varieties have flesh that is sweet and soft like butter.

No-Bake Strawberry Cream Pie

Decorate this cake with fresh berries, if desired.

1	tub (425 g) frozen strawberries in sugar or syrup, thawed	1
1	package (250 g) cream cheese, softened	1
1/3 cup	granulated sugar	75 mL
1 tsp	vanilla	5 mL
1 tsp	lemon juice	5 mL
1/4 cup	orange juice	50 mL
1	envelope (1 tbsp/15 mL) unflavoured gelatin	1
2 cups	frozen whipped topping, thawed	500 mL
1	(170 g) ready-to-use graham cracker or chocolate crumb crust	1

Strain juice from strawberries, discard. Mash strawberries well to make about 2/3 cup (150 mL).

In a large bowl, using electric mixer beat cream cheese with sugar, vanilla and lemon juice until very smooth. Beat in strawberries, scraping beaters often.

Pour orange juice into a small saucepan. Sprinkle gelatin over juice and let stand 3 minutes to soften. Stir over low heat until gelatin is dissolved. Beat orange juice mixture into cream cheese mixture. Chill briefly until cream cheese mixture just begins to mound.

Gently fold in whipped topping until well blended. Spoon into prepared crust. Chill until set, 2 to 3 hours or overnight.

Makes 6 servings.

Per serving: cal 429, pro 6 g, fat 27 g, carb 43 g, fibre 1 g

Tasty Tidbit

When combining gelatin and liquid be sure to add the gelatin to the liquid and not the other way around. The gelatin needs to be added slowly so that it doesn't clump.

Individual Baked Alaskas

Look in the bakery section or the produce section near the berries of your grocery store for sponge cake shells, about 3 inches (7.5 cm) in diameter.

2	sponge cake shells	2
1/4 cup	seedless raspberry jam or jelly	50 mL
3	egg whites	3
1/8 tsp	salt	0.5 mL
1/3 cup	sugar	75 mL
2	scoops ice cream, any flavour	2

Place shells on double layer of brown paper or foil, shiny side down, on a wooden board or baking sheet. Spread inside of cake shells with jam or jelly.

Beat egg whites with salt until fluffy, then gradually add sugar, beating until egg whites are stiff.

Spoon one scoop of ice cream into the hollow of each cake shell. Spread meringue over entire surface of ice cream and cake sides.

Bake in preheated 500°F (250°C) oven until meringue is lightly browned, about 5 minutes; watch carefully. Slide a lifter under each cake to place on serving plate. Serve immediately.

Makes 2 servings.

Per serving: cal 422, pro 8 g, fat 6 g, carb 86 g, fibre 1 g

Tips
- Individual desserts can be made ahead and frozen, then wrapped and stored in a cake box or plastic container in the freezer. These may be baked directly from the frozen state.
- Recipe may be doubled.
- If you cannot find sponge cake shells, use 2 slices of pound cake instead.

Tasty Tidbit
When beating the egg whites for the meringue, use a glass bowl instead of plastic, so that the egg whites fluff up to a greater volume.

CHAPTER 4

Sore Mouth *and* Swallowing Problems

INTRODUCTION

If you are receiving radiation to the head, neck or esophagus, you may experience a sore mouth or throat. Some chemotherapy drugs can also affect your ability to chew and swallow. The recipes and suggestions in this chapter will give you ideas of foods and drinks that may make it easier to eat during this time.

Radiation to the head and neck area and some medications can leave your mouth feeling very dry. It may be easier to stick to soups and very moist foods for a while. Sometimes drinking thin liquids like water can be harder than drinking something that is thicker like a milkshake. If this is happening to you, check out the recipes for milkshakes, smoothies and puddings in this chapter.

Radiation treatment can change your saliva. It may become thick and ropy. Using baking soda mouthwash or flat soda water will help to clean your mouth and remove the thick saliva. Gargle before and after eating, as well as between meals.

RECIPE FOR BAKING SODA MOUTHWASH

| 1 tsp | baking soda | 5 mL |
| 12 - 16 oz | warm water | 375 - 500 mL |

Mix well. Discard after 24 hours.

HELPFUL HINTS FOR YOU

- Use extra gravy and sauces with meat, potatoes, rice or pasta.
- Dip bread in soup or gravy.
- Try fruit nectar such as peach or pear instead of juice. Dilute the nectar with water, if you find it too sweet or thick.
- Let cold cereals soak in milk to soften them.
- Dip cookies in warm milk or hot drinks.
- Sip liquids with your meals to help you swallow.
- Drink shakes made with milk and ice cream or soymilk and yogurt.
- Avoid acidic and spicy foods, as they may irritate your mouth and throat.
- Avoid commercial mouthwash, as it contains alcohol and can dry out your mouth.

HELPFUL HINTS FOR THE CAREGIVER

- Add milk and butter or margarine to mashed vegetables and potatoes.
- Cook pastas until soft and mix with cream sauce.
- Add tofu to soups and casseroles for extra protein.
- Cook hot cereal with milk instead of water and add butter or margarine and sugar.
- Mash, mince or purée foods to make them easier to swallow.
- Make a new batch of baking soda mouthwash in the morning. Leave some by the sink in the washroom and place some in a bottle for outings.
- Keep a few jars of baby food meat on hand. It is a quick and easy way to add protein to soups and stews.

How to Modify a Meal Plan

AVERAGE DAY	DAY WITH SORE MOUTH AND THROAT
Breakfast	**Breakfast**
Corn Flakes®	Cream of Wheat®
	with brown sugar and applesauce
2% milk	whole milk
2 slices toast	soft poached egg
with peanut butter and jam	
orange juice	pear nectar
coffee	café au lait
Lunch	**Lunch**
corn beef sandwich	cream of mushroom soup
on rye bread	
Greek salad	macaroni and cheese
	with extra sauce and cheese
soft drink	vanilla milkshake
	Afternoon Snack
	vanilla pudding
Dinner	**Dinner**
2 pork chops	poached fish with sauce
baked potato	whipped potatoes
	with whole milk and butter
sliced carrots	mashed squash
broccoli spears	chopped green beans
apple pie	ice cream
with ice cream	with puréed peaches
coffee	café au lait
Evening Snack	**Evening Snack**
chips and dip	mango smoothie
soft drink	

Sample Menu

Use baking soda mouthwash before and after eating.

This sample menu is intended to ease chewing and swallowing as well as provide protein and calories. It does not represent a well balanced diet.

Breakfast
Peach nectar
Applesauce mixed with yogurt
Creamy Maple Oatmeal*
Milk
Weak tea

Lunch
Cream of mushroom soup
Soft Scrambled Eggs*
Peanut Butter Mousse*
Milk
Water

Afternoon Snack
Banana Smoothie*

Dinner
Bean and Lentil Vegetable Soup*
Pasta in Cheese Sauce*
Mashed carrots with butter
Tofu Tiramisù*
Milk
Water

Evening Snack
Easy Baked Custard**

* Recipes are from Chapter 4 – *Sore Mouth and Swallowing Problems*.
** Recipe from Chapter 1 – *Loss of Appetite*.

Recipe Index

CROSSOVER RECIPES

Banana Smoothie

For a peach smoothie, substitute 3/4 cup (175 mL) drained canned peaches for the banana.

1 1/2 cups	milk, high-protein milk, or cream	375 mL
1	ripe banana, cut into chunks	1
1 tbsp	honey	15 mL
1/4 tsp	cinnamon	1 mL

In blender, purée all ingredients until smooth.

Makes 2 servings.

Per serving (1 cup/250 mL): cal 176, pro 7 g, fat 4 g, carb 31 g, fibre 1 g

Tips
- Pour over ice, if desired.
- To make high-protein milk, pour 2 cups (500 mL) of homogenized milk into a bottle or a jar with a lid. Add 1/2 cup (125 mL) skim milk powder, screw on lid and shake until milk powder dissolves. Refrigerate before using.

Tasty Tidbit
Bananas are high in potassium, magnesium and contain dietary fibre. Adding bananas to smoothies provides a sweet and creamy texture.

Vanilla Berry Smoothie

For easier blending, let berries partially thaw before puréeing.

1/2 cup	vanilla soy beverage or milk	125 mL
1/2 cup	peach or mango nectar	125 mL
2 cups	frozen strawberries or blueberries	500 mL

In blender, purée all ingredients until smooth.

Makes 2 servings.

Per serving (1 cup): cal 126, pro 3 g, fat 1 g, carb 28 g, fibre 3 g

Tip
• If using milk, add 1/4 tsp (1 mL) vanilla.

Tasty Tidbit
Soy beverage is an excellent alternative to milk in any recipe. It is a great choice for those who cannot tolerate lactose (the natural sugar in milk). For extra nutrition, choose varieties that are fortified with calcium and vitamin D.

Vanilla Milkshake

Simple and quick. Vary it by using different flavours of smooth ice cream such as butterscotch or chocolate. Avoid ice cream with nuts or chunks.

1 cup	milk, high-protein milk or light cream	250 mL
2	scoops vanilla ice cream	2
1/4 tsp	vanilla	1 mL

In blender, purée all ingredients until smooth.

Makes about 1 1/2 cups (375 mL).

Per serving (1 cup/250 mL): cal 151, pro 6 g, fat 7 g, carb 16 g, fibre 0 g

Tips

- There are as many as four types of cream in the dairy case and they vary in fat content, noted on the label by MF (milk fat). Light cream is 5% MF, half and half cream is 10%, table cream 18%, and whipping cream 35%. The higher fat creams are also thicker in consistency.

- To make high-protein milk, pour 2 cups (500 mL) of homogenized milk into a bottle or a jar with a lid. Add 1/2 cup (125 mL) skim milk powder, screw on lid and shake until milk powder dissolves. Refrigerate before using.

Tasty Tidbit

Vanilla is a flavouring agent and comes as an extract, powder or whole bean. Good quality vanilla has a strong aromatic flavour but is expensive. If cost is an issue, use artificial vanilla flavouring.

Maple Milkshake

*This milkshake takes only minutes to prepare and offers a great maple flavour.
For a thinner version, substitute skim milk and frozen yogurt for the milk and
ice cream.*

2 cups	milk, high-protein milk, or light cream	500 mL
4	scoops vanilla ice cream	4
1/2 cup	maple syrup	125 mL

In blender, purée all ingredients until smooth.

Makes about 3 1/2 cups (875 mL).

Per serving (1 cup/250 mL): cal 336, pro 8 g, fat 10 g, carb 57 g, fibre 0 g

Tip
• To make high-protein milk, pour 2 cups (500 mL) of homogenized milk into a
  bottle or a jar with a lid. Add 1/2 cup (125 mL) skim milk powder, screw on lid and
  shake until milk powder dissolves. Refrigerate before using.

Tasty Tidbit
Maple syrup is one of the most delicious, all-Canadian ways to satisfy a sweet tooth.
The characteristic colour and flavour come from boiling the sap from the maple tree
long enough for the water to evaporate and leave the sweet and wonderful syrup.

Banana Split Shake

A triple treat with three flavours in one shake.

1 cup	milk or high-protein milk	250 mL
1/2 cup	sliced strawberries	125 mL
1	ripe banana, cut into chunks	1
2 tbsp	chocolate powder drink mix	25 mL
1 - 2 tsp	granulated sugar	5 - 10 mL

In blender, purée all ingredients until smooth.

Makes 2 servings.

Per serving (1 cup/250 mL): cal 171, pro 5 g, fat 3 g, carb 34 g, fibre 2 g

Tips
- If you don't have fresh strawberries, use frozen. Just let berries partially thaw before tossing in blender.
- To make high-protein milk, pour 2 cups (500 mL) of homogenized milk into a bottle or a jar with a lid. Add 1/2 cup (125 mL) skim milk powder, screw on lid and shake until milk powder dissolves. Refrigerate before using.

Tasty Tidbit
Strawberries added to a milkshake not only add flavour, they also add dietary fibre and vitamin C.

CREAMY MAPLE OATMEAL

1 1/4 cups	milk, high-protein milk, or light cream	300 mL
1 cup	quick-cooking (not instant) rolled oats	250 mL
1/4 cup	maple syrup	50 mL
1/2 cup	plain yogurt	125 mL

In saucepan, bring milk to a boil over medium heat. Stir in oats and maple syrup and return to a boil. Reduce heat to medium-low and cook for 1 minute. Stir in yogurt. Serve warm with a few spoonfuls of milk, if desired.

Makes 3 servings.

Per serving: cal 270, pro 10 g, fat 5 g, carb 48 g, fibre 3 g

TIP
- To make high-protein milk, pour 2 cups (500 mL) of homogenized milk into a bottle or a jar with a lid. Add 1/2 cup (125 mL) skim milk powder, screw on lid and shake until milk powder dissolves. Refrigerate before using.

TASTY TIDBIT
Whether it is called oatmeal in North America or porridge across the Atlantic, this hot cereal is a great comfort food. Have it as a nutritious meal – anytime!

Soft Scrambled Eggs

2	eggs	2
2 tbsp	water	25 mL
1/4 tsp	salt	1 mL
pinch	pepper	pinch
1 tsp	butter or margarine	5 mL

Lightly whisk eggs with water, salt and pepper.

Heat a small skillet over medium-high heat. Melt butter in skillet. Pour in egg mixture and immediately reduce heat to medium-low. As mixture begins to set, gently move spatula across bottom and sides of skillet to form large, soft curds. Cook until eggs are thickened but still moist, about 2 minutes.

Makes 1 serving.

Per serving: cal 179, pro 12 g, fat 14 g, carb 1 g, fibre 0 g

Tasty Tidbit

One of the quickest and easiest ways to cook eggs is scrambled. Don't overcook or use high heat as the eggs will become rubbery!

Puréed Vegetable Soup

It takes just a little time and effort to make a basic soup base. To the base, add steamed broccoli florets, peas or cooked red peppers, as desired. Garnish with chopped parsley or cilantro.

2	medium potatoes peeled and cut into chunks	2
1	carrot, diced	1
1	medium onion, chopped	1
1	clove garlic, minced	1
4 cups	vegetable broth	1 L
pinch	dried thyme leaves	pinch

In large saucepan, combine potatoes, carrot, onion, garlic, vegetable broth and thyme. Bring to a boil, cover and simmer until vegetables are very tender about 20 to 25 minutes.

With an immersion blender or in a blender or food processor, purée until smooth.

Makes about 5 cups (1.25 L).

Per serving (1 cup/250 mL): cal 69, pro 2 g, fat 1 g, carb 14 g, fibre 2 g

Tip

- An immersion blender is a handy appliance for smooth soups and sauces. The soup can be puréed right in the pot. Just be sure to hold it vertical with the blade in the bottom of the soup before turning it on.

Tasty Tidbit

The sulphur compound in onions is responsible for the characteristic aroma and flavour of the onion but it can also make us cry when we cut them. To reduce tears when cooking with onions either chill the onion in the freezer for 5 minutes prior to slicing or keep the root intact when cutting or peeling.

Bean and Lentil Vegetable Soup

This soup uses the Puréed Vegetable Soup (page 117) as the base. Canned beans are a great pantry staple, so much easier than cooking and soaking dry beans.

5 cups	puréed vegetable soup (page 117)	1.25 L
1	can (19 oz/540 mL) white or red kidney beans, drained and rinsed	1
1/4 cup	dried red lentils, rinsed	50 mL
	salt and pepper	
	chopped fresh parsley	

In large saucepan, bring vegetable soup to a simmer over medium heat.

Add drained beans and lentils. Return to a simmer, reduce heat and simmer for 10 to 15 minutes or until beans are tender, stirring occasionally.

With an immersion blender or in a blender or food processor, purée until smooth. Add water, if necessary, for desired consistency. Season with salt and pepper to taste. Garnish with chopped parsley.

Makes about 6 cups (1.5 L).

Per serving (1 1/2 cup/375 mL): cal 251, pro 13 g, fat 1 g, carb 48 g, fibre 13 g

Tasty Tidbit

Beans and lentils are part of the legume family, also known as pulses. Their increased popularity is thanks to their high-protein, high-fibre and low-fat content. They pair well with many flavours and spices and are an excellent addition to soups and stews.

Souper Easy Tuna and Noodles

1 tbsp	butter or margarine	15 mL
2 tbsp	all-purpose flour	25 mL
1	can (10 oz/284 mL) chicken noodle soup	1
1/2 cup	milk	125 mL
1	can (170 g) flaked tuna, drained	1

In saucepan, melt butter over medium heat. Stir in flour to make a paste. Stir in chicken noodle soup and milk, stirring constantly until mixture comes to a boil and thickens.

Stir in tuna until heated through.

Makes about 2 cups (500 mL).

Per serving (1 cup/250 mL): cal 269, pro 23 g, fat 10 g, carb 20 g, fibre 1 g

Tasty Tidbit

Tuna is terrific! Rich in protein, low in cost and versatile in the kitchen – add it to casseroles, salads and sandwiches. When buying canned tuna, go for light instead of white for greater economy.

Pasta in Cheese Sauce

Any small pasta works well in this creamy "mac and cheese."

1 cup	small shell pasta	250 mL
2 tbsp	butter	25 mL
2 tbsp	all-purpose flour	25 mL
1 1/2 cups	milk, high-protein milk or half and half cream salt and pepper	375 mL
1 cup	shredded Cheddar cheese	250 mL

Cook pasta in boiling salted water until tender, about 7 to 8 minutes.

Meanwhile, in small heavy saucepan melt butter over low heat. Whisk in flour and cook for 2 minutes. Gradually whisk in milk and cook until mixture comes to a boil and thickens. Stir in cheese until melted.

Drain pasta and stir into sauce. Season to taste with salt and pepper.

Makes 2 servings.

Per serving: cal 619, pro 27 g, fat 35 g, carb 50 g, fibre 2 g

Tips
- If chewing is difficult, use small pasta such as orzo or pastina.
- For a simple sauce, heat a pourable cheese sauce in the microwave and pour over pasta.
- Sauces are a breeze to make in the microwave. Here's how: in microwavable bowl, melt butter. Stir in flour, then gradually whisk in milk until smooth. Microwave 2 minutes on medium. Stir well and microwave 2 to 3 minutes on medium until sauces comes to a boil and thickens. Stir in cheese until melted.
- To make high-protein milk, pour 2 cups (500 mL) of homogenized milk into a bottle or a jar with a lid. Add 1/2 cup (125 mL) skim milk powder, screw on lid and shake until milk powder dissolves. Refrigerate before using.

Tasty Tidbit
Cheese, milk and yogurt are excellent sources of protein, calcium and vitamin A. Calcium is especially important for bone strength and helps to reduce the risk of osteoporosis.

Moroccan Tofu Stew

1	package (400 g) firm tofu	1
1/4 cup	soy sauce	50 mL
3 tbsp	smooth peanut butter	45 mL
2 cups	vegetable broth	500 mL
1	medium onion, diced	1
4	cloves garlic, minced	4
1 tsp	ground cumin	5 mL
1/2 tsp	each, mild paprika & cinnamon	2 mL
1/4 tsp	turmeric	1 mL
1	medium sweet potato, peeled & cubed, about 2 1/2 cups (625 mL)	1
2	medium zucchini, cubed, about 2 1/2 cups (625 mL)	2
1/2 cup	chopped, bottled or canned roasted red pepper	125 mL
1/3 cup	seedless raisins	75 mL

Rinse tofu, wrap in a clean dishtowel and place under a plate for 10 minutes to squeeze out excess moisture. Cut into 1/2-inch (1 cm) cubes. Whisk soy sauce and peanut butter together. Add tofu to soy mixture in a zip closure bag or bowl and marinate for 1 hour or more in the refrigerator.

In a large saucepan over medium-high heat, heat vegetable broth. Add onion, garlic and spices and cook for 2 minutes.

Add all remaining ingredients except for marinating tofu and mix. Bring to a boil, then reduce heat to simmer, covered for 15 minutes.

Stir in tofu and marinade, and simmer, uncovered over medium heat until heated through.

Makes 4 servings.

Per serving: cal 323, pro 16 g, fat 12 g, carb 45 g, fibre 6 g

Tip
- If your mouth is very sore or chewing is difficult, purée the stew using a blender, immersion blender or food processor.

Tasty Tidbit
Tofu, made from bean curd, is bland but highly absorbent. The magic of this is that it can take on the flavours of your favourite stews, casseroles or stir-frys. Use it for some extra protein in a vegetarian entrée.

Sweet Potato Maple Mash

As an alternative, try mashed squash or rutabaga instead of sweet potatoes.

3	medium sweet potatoes, about 1 1/2 lbs (750 g)	3
2 tbsp	maple syrup	25 mL
1/4 cup	melted butter or margarine	50 mL
1/4 cup	milk or high-protein milk	50 mL

Scrub potatoes and bake, unpeeled, in preheated 325°F (160°C) oven for 45 to 60 minutes, or until tender. When cool enough to handle, peel and mash.

In large bowl, combine mashed sweet potatoes, maple syrup, butter and milk. Serve warm.

Makes 4 servings.

Per serving: cal 272, pro 3 g, fat 12 g, carb 40 g, fibre 4 g

Tips

• To microwave, pierce in several places with a sharp knife and arrange on paper towel. Microwave on high for 6 to 8 minutes or until potatoes are tender. Let stand 10 minutes. Peel potatoes while still warm.

• To make high-protein milk, pour 2 cups (500 mL) of homogenized milk into a bottle or a jar with a lid. Add 1/2 cup (125 mL) skim milk powder, screw on lid and shake until milk powder dissolves. Refrigerate before using.

Tasty Tidbit

Sweet potatoes are a great source of vitamin A – the vitamin important for growth, healthy skin and night vision. This sweet potato recipe provides a sweet contrast to savoury spices.

Easy Butterscotch Mousse

Substitute vanilla, chocolate or banana pudding for a different flavour.

1	package (113 g) instant butterscotch pudding mix	1
1 1/2 cups	milk or high-protein milk	375 mL
2 cups	frozen whipped topping, thawed	500 mL

Prepare the pudding according to package directions, using 1 1/2 cups (375 mL) milk instead of 2 cups (500 mL) suggested on package.

Gently fold in whipped topping. Cover and refrigerate until set, about 30 minutes.

Makes 8 servings.

Per serving (1/2 cup/125 mL): cal 120, pro 2 g, fat 5 g, carb 18 g, fibre 0 g

Tip
• To make high-protein milk, pour 2 cups (500 mL) of homogenized milk into a bottle or a jar with a lid. Add 1/2 cup (125 mL) skim milk powder, screw on lid and shake until milk powder dissolves. Refrigerate before using.

Tasty Tidbit
Two of the world's most complementary ingredients – butter and sugar – come together to form an outstanding pudding flavour – *butterscotch!* This pudding makes an excellent dessert, but can also make a great midday snack.

Peanut Butter Mousse

This make-ahead dessert is a bit of an effort, but worth it. Preparing individual servings means you can take out just the number of servings you need from the freezer.

1 cup	whipping cream	250 mL
1 cup	plain full fat (3 - 4% MF) yogurt	250 mL
3/4 cup	smooth peanut butter	175 mL
1 cup	granulated sugar	250 mL
1/2 cup	milk or high-protein milk	125 mL

In bowl, whip cream until firm.

In another bowl, combine yogurt, peanut butter, sugar and milk. With an electric mixer, beat mixture on low speed, gradually increasing speed to high. Scrape down the sides of the bowl with a spatula.

Gently fold whipped cream into peanut butter mixture until combined.

Spoon into individual serving dishes. Cover and refrigerate for 2 to 3 hours or until set. For longer storage, freeze.

Makes about 8 servings.

Per serving (2/3 cup/150 mL): cal 367, pro 9 g, fat 24 g, carb 33 g, fibre 1 g

Tip
• To make high-protein milk, pour 2 cups (500 mL) of homogenized milk into a bottle or a jar with a lid. Add 1/2 cup (125 mL) skim milk powder, screw on lid and shake until milk powder dissolves. Refrigerate before using.

Tasty Tidbit
Making your own whipped cream allows you to control the amount of sugar that goes into the product. Chilling the cream, bowl and beaters makes it easier to whip.

Soft Vanilla Pudding

1/2 cup	granulated sugar	125 mL
2 tbsp	cornstarch	25 mL
2 cups	milk	500 mL
2	eggs, lightly beaten	2
1 tbsp	butter or margarine	15 mL
1 tsp	vanilla	5 mL

In heavy saucepan, combine sugar and cornstarch. Whisk in milk. Cook, stirring constantly over medium heat until mixture just comes to a boil and begins to thicken.

Remove pan from heat. Gently whisk about 1 cup (250 mL) hot milk mixture into beaten eggs to warm them up. Whisk egg mixture into milk mixture and return pan to heat over medium-low heat. Cook until thickened, whisking or stirring constantly to prevent burning. Do not boil.

Remove from heat and stir in butter and vanilla until butter melts. Pour into dessert cups. Cool at room temperature and serve warm, or refrigerate about 2 hours to serve chilled.

Makes 5 servings.

Per serving (1/2 cup/125 mL): cal 190, pro 6 g, fat 6 g, carb 28 g, fibre 0 g

Variations
- To make Coffee Pudding, stir 2 tsp (10 mL) instant coffee granules into sugar and cornstarch mixture. Continue as above.
- To make Butterscotch Pudding, use dark brown sugar in place of granulated sugar and increase butter to 2 tbsp (25 mL).

Tasty Tidbit
This recipe uses eggs and cornstarch as the main thickeners. When egg is mixed with liquid (like milk) and heated, it thickens the liquid as it cooks. Pudding made with eggs is also called "custard." Care should be taken to maintain a steady, even temperature throughout the cooking process.

CREAMY RICE PUDDING

1/2 cup	water	125 mL
1/2 cup	instant rice	125 mL
1 3/4 cups	milk	425 mL
2 tbsp	granulated sugar	25 mL
1/4 tsp	salt	1 mL
1	egg	1
1 tsp	vanilla	5 mL
1/2 tsp	nutmeg or cinnamon	2 mL

In saucepan, bring water to a boil and stir in rice. Remove from heat, cover and let stand 5 minutes.

Stir in milk, sugar and salt and bring to a boil over medium heat, stirring constantly. Reduce heat and simmer, uncovered for 5 minutes, stirring occasionally.

In bowl, whisk egg, vanilla and nutmeg together. Gradually stir a small amount of hot rice mixture into beaten egg, mixing well. Blend egg mixture into hot rice mixture in saucepan. Cook and stir over low heat for 1 minute. Do not boil. Remove from heat and immediately pour into dessert dishes or serving bowl.

Makes 4 servings.

Per serving (1/2 cup/125 mL): cal 145, pro 6 g, fat 4 g, carb 22 g, fibre 0 g

TIP
- To heat a leftover serving of cold rice pudding, simply microwave on medium for 20 to 30 seconds.

TASTY TIDBIT
The creamy texture of rice pudding comes from cooking the rice slowly with milk and sugar on the stovetop. After a while, the starch from the rice breaks down and creates that famous smooth consistency. Try a drizzle of maple syrup and a sprinkle of cinnamon as a tasty garnish.

Raspberry Whip

Change the flavour of this easy dessert by changing the flavour of the jelly powder.

1	package (85 g) raspberry or strawberry jelly powder	1
1 cup	boiling water	250 mL
2 cups	vanilla ice cream	500 mL

In heatproof bowl, pour boiling water over jelly powder and stir until completely dissolved. Briefly cool in refrigerator, about 10 minutes.

Meanwhile spoon ice cream into a 2-cup (500 mL) measure. Whisk ice cream into jelly, a large spoonful at a time until well blended.

Divide mixture into four dessert dishes. Chill in refrigerator until set, about 20 minutes.

Makes 4 servings.

Per serving (3/4 cup/175 mL): cal 214, pro 4 g, fat 7 g, carb 35 g

Tasty Tidbit
Gelatin dessert is referred to as jelly in the U.K. and Australia. In Canada and the U.S. it is usually referred to by the brand name JELL-O.®

Jelly Parfait

1	package (85 g) peach or strawberry jelly powder	1
1 cup	boiling water	250 mL
2 cups	ice cubes	500 mL
1/2 cup	plain or fruit yogurt	125 mL

In heatproof bowl, pour boiling water over jelly powder and stir until completely dissolved. Add ice cubes and stir until jelly begins to thicken and ice is partially melted (bowl will feel cool). Remove unmelted ice with a slotted spoon.

Distribute half of the jelly mixture among four dessert dishes. Chill briefly.

Whisk remaining jelly until foamy. Continue whisking jelly while gradually adding yogurt. When thick and pale, spoon over clear layer of jelly in dishes. Chill 15 to 20 minutes.

Makes 4 servings.

Per serving (1/2 cup/125 mL): cal 99, pro 3 g, fat 0 g, carb 21 g, fibre 0 g

Tip
• If desired, diced canned peaches or crushed strawberries can be spooned into dishes before clear jelly is added.

Tasty Tidbit
The first jelly dessert came to stores in 1897, manufactured by the Genessee Pure Food Company. Its popularity grew following World War II, with an increased demand for foods that were convenient and easy to prepare. To this day, jelly continues to be a popular comfort food!

Tofu Tiramisù, p.130

Tofu Pumpkin Pudding

A 14 oz/398 mL can of pumpkin purée (not pumpkin pie filling) is perfect for this creamy pumpkin pudding.

1	package (300 g) soft or silken tofu	1
1 1/2 cups	cooked pumpkin puree	375 mL
2/3 cup	brown sugar	150 mL
1/2 tsp	cinnamon	2 mL
1/2 tsp	salt	2 mL
1/2 tsp	vanilla	2 mL
1/4 tsp	ginger	1 mL

Combine all ingredients in a blender or food processor and blend until smooth. Divide into 4 serving bowls. Chill about 1 hour.

Makes 4 servings.

Per serving (3/4 cup/175 mL): cal 213, pro 5 g, fat 2 g, carb 46 g, fibre 3 g

Tasty Tidbit
Soft and silken tofu are creamy, custard-like products that can be used in smoothies, soups, puddings and dressings. Tofu is a great source of vegetarian protein.

Chicken, Rice and Mushroom Sauté, p.147

Tofu Tiramisù

Silken tofu and meringue powder replace mascarpone and raw egg whites in this take on tiramisù. No one will guess tofu is in this creamy Italian classic.

2	eggs	2
1/4 cup	granulated sugar	50 mL
4 tsp	meringue powder (or equivalent to 2 egg whites)	20 mL
1/4 cup	water	50 mL
1	package (300 g) silken soft tofu	1
1/4 cup	hot water	50 mL
1 tsp	instant coffee granules	5 mL
1 tsp	rum extract	5 mL
18 - 20	ladyfingers (Savoiardi biscuits)	18 - 20
1 tsp	unsweetened cocoa	5 mL

In mixing bowl with electric mixer, beat eggs and sugar until thickened and pale yellow, 3 to 4 minutes.

In heavy saucepan over low heat, cook egg mixture, whisking to prevent curdling, until slightly thickened. Do not boil. Set aside to cool to room temperature.

Using clean beaters, beat meringue powder with 1/4 cup (50 mL) water until stiff peaks forms. Set aside.

In large bowl, mash and whisk drained tofu until smooth. Whisk in egg custard. Fold in meringue.

In small bowl, mix 1/4 cup (50 mL) hot water and instant coffee, stirring to dissolve. Stir in rum extract. Pour into a shallow dish.

Dip both sides of ladyfingers into coffee mixture and arrange 9 to 10 ladyfingers in one layer in bottom of an 8-inch (2 L) glass square dish, cutting to fit as necessary. Spoon half of custard mixture over ladyfingers. Repeat with a second layer of ladyfingers and custard.

Place cocoa in small sieve and shake evenly over top. Cover and refrigerate a few hours or overnight.

Makes 6 servings.

Per serving: cal 213, pro 9 g, fat 6 g, carb 30 g, fibre 0 g

Tasty Tidbit

Tiramisù means "pick-me-up" in Italian. Letting this recipe sit overnight gives the flavours a chance to blend and achieve their optimal balance. *Nothing beats this great smooth taste!*

CHAPTER 5

Dealing *with* Diarrhea

Introduction

Diarrhea is a common side effect of treatment for many types of cancer. The cause may be certain chemotherapy drugs, radiation to the abdomen or pelvis area, surgery, or medications such as antibiotics. The recipes in this chapter are helpful when you are experiencing gastrointestinal upset and diarrhea. They focus on foods that are low in insoluble fibre, lactose, caffeine, fat, and spices. It is important to remember that when you have severe diarrhea, it can be challenging to meet your daily needs. Focus on staying well hydrated during this time. Aim for at least 8 cups (2 L) of fluid per day to prevent dehydration.

Many people find the term "fibre" confusing so we thought it would be helpful to provide an explanation for you. Dietary fibre is the part of the plant that passes through the body without being digested. There are two types of dietary fibre: *insoluble* and *soluble*. *Insoluble* fibre is found in foods such as whole-grain breads and cereals, skins of fruits and vegetables, as well as seeds and nuts. It can make diarrhea worse. For this reason, we recommend that you focus on choosing white breads and cereals made from refined grains. *Soluble* fibre found in oatmeal and bananas dissolves in water to form a gel and may help control diarrhea.

You will notice that many of the recipes in this cookbook are made with lactose-free milk. Lactose is a type of sugar that is found naturally in milk and milk products. During treatments such as chemotherapy and radiation to the abdomen/pelvis area, you may have difficulty digesting lactose. Lactose-free milk and soy beverages, found in the dairy section of the grocery store, are good alternatives. Other milk products that are often well tolerated include low-fat yogurt (without seeds), and low-fat hard cheese.

HERE ARE SOME FOODS THAT MAY BE BETTER TOLERATED IF YOU HAVE DIARRHEA:

Meats and Alternatives:	all lean meats and fish prepared with small amount of fat tuna or salmon packed in water, smooth peanut butter (in small amounts)
Milk:	lactose-free milk or soy beverage low-fat yogurt without seeds (<2% MF) low-fat cheese (<20% MF)
Grains:	breads and crackers made with white flour cereals made with refined grains such as puffed rice, Corn Flakes,® and Cream of Wheat® white rice and pasta noodles arrowroot, social tea and oatmeal cookies
Fruits:*	melons, peeled apples and applesauce, bananas, and oranges without the membranes
Vegetables:*	cooked carrots, green or yellow beans, asparagus tips, mushrooms and peeled white potatoes

* Limit serving size to 1/2 cup (125 mL) or 1 small fruit.

HELPFUL HINTS FOR YOU

- Avoid dried peas and beans such as lentils, kidney beans and chickpeas.
- Limit use of hot spices such as chili powders, curry and hot peppers.
- Cut back on drinks containing caffeine such as coffee, strong tea and cola. Choose decaffeinated versions of these drinks or teas such as chamomile instead.
- Drink lots of fluids to prevent dehydration. Good fluid choices include JELL-O®, popsicles, broth soup and flat ginger ale.
- Try drinking your liquids at room temperature as they are often easier to tolerate than when they are very hot or very cold.
- Limit intake of high-fat, greasy foods such as those that have been fried or contain creams.
- Eat fewer fruits and vegetables and choose juices instead. Dilute juices with water if they are too sweet.
- Try to drink an additional cup of fluid for every episode of diarrhea/loose bowel movement you have.
- Keep a diary of your diet and of your bowel movements. This may help identify problem foods for you.

HELPFUL HINTS FOR THE CAREGIVER

- Allow soups to cool down before serving.
- Keep track of how much fluid your loved one is drinking to make sure they don't get dehydrated.
- Peel fruits such as apples before serving to your loved one.
- Stock snack foods such as plain crackers, JELL-O®, white bread, and applesauce in your home for easy access.
- Use cooking methods such as baking, broiling and steaming instead of deep-frying.
- Use broths to flavour and moisten foods instead of cream sauces.

How to Modify a Meal Plan

AVERAGE DAY	DAY WHEN HAVING DIARRHEA
Breakfast	**Breakfast**
1/2 cup of 2% milk	1/2 cup of lactose-free 2% milk
1 cup of Raisin Bran®	1 cup of Rice Krispies®
1/2 cup of blueberries	1/2 banana
1 cup of coffee	1 cup decaffeinated tea
	Morning Snack
	1 cup diluted apple juice
	(1/2 cup water/1/2 cup juice)
Lunch	**Lunch**
2 slices of multigrain bread	2 slices of white bread
1 tbsp of mayonnaise	1 tsp mustard
3 slices of turkey	3 slices of turkey
2 tomato slices	
1 cup of cream of broccoli soup	1 cup of chicken noodle soup
1 cup chocolate milk	1 cup lactose-free 2% milk
Afternoon Snack	**Afternoon Snack**
1 medium apple	1/2 cup of applesauce
	Afternoon Drink
	1 cup water
Dinner	**Dinner**
3 oz meat	3 oz meat
baked potato	1 cup of white rice
1 cup of salad	
1/2 cup of broccoli	1/2 cup of cooked carrots
1 cup of 2% milk	1 cup of lactose-free 2% milk
Evening Snack	**Evening Snack**
1 cup popcorn	1 cup pretzels
1 cup of cola drink	1 cup of ginger ale
TOTAL FIBRE = 30 grams	TOTAL FIBRE = 7 grams
	23 grams less
TOTAL FAT = 39 grams	TOTAL FAT = 24 grams
	15 grams less

Sample Menu

This sample menu is low in fruits and vegetables, as many of them are not well tolerated when you have diarrhea. It does not represent a well balanced diet.

Breakfast
Banana Oatmeal*
Lactose-free milk

Morning Snack
Applesauce
Refreshing Orange Tea*

Lunch
Chicken Broth*
Turkey slices on white toast
Soy Pudding*

Afternoon. Snack
Diluted fruit juice
Easy Pretzel-Style Bun*

Dinner
Lemony Baked Fish*
Carrots with Zip*
Cooked white rice
Water

Evening Snack
Cinnamon Apple Tea Cooler*
Banana Bread*

* Recipes are from Chapter 5 – *Dealing with Diarrhea.*

RECIPE INDEX

CROSSOVER RECIPES

Refreshing Orange Tea

Make this with a lemon zinger tea and it's a refreshing lemon-orange combination.

2 cups	freshly brewed herbal or decaffeinated tea	500 mL
1/4 cup	orange juice (pulp-free) or peach nectar	50 mL

Cool tea, stir in orange juice and serve warm or cold. Sweeten to taste with either sugar or sugar substitute, up to 2 tsp (10 mL) per cup (250 mL).

Makes about 2 servings.

Per serving (1 cup/250 mL): cal 16, pro 0 g, fat 0 g, carb 4 g, fibre 0 g

Tip
• If orange juice is too acidic, try peach nectar.

Tasty Tidbit
Did you know that orange juice is a source of potassium, a mineral that can be lost when you have diarrhea? Other good sources of potassium are bananas, cantaloupe and potatoes.

Cinnamon Apple Tea Cooler

This makes a refreshing, tart tea with a hint of cinnamon. Store in refrigerator for up to 3 days.

6	cinnamon apple herbal tea bags	6
1 1/2 cups	boiling water	375 mL
1 1/2 cups	cold water	375 mL
1 cup	cranberry cocktail or cranberry juice	250 mL
1 tsp	lemon juice	5 mL

In heatproof container, pour boiling water over tea bags. Cover and let stand 4 minutes. Remove tea bags, let cool.

In pitcher, combine tea, cold water and juices. Cover and refrigerate until ready to use. Sweeten to taste with either sugar or sugar substitute.

Makes 4 servings.

Per serving (1 cup/250 mL): cal 37, pro 0 g, fat 0 g, carb 9 g, fibre 0 g

Tasty Tidbit

Did you know that cinnamon is the inner bark of a tropical evergreen tree, known for its spicy, delicate flavour? Cinnamon sticks steeped in boiled water can impart as much flavour as a tea bag.

Banana Oatmeal

2 cups	peach or apricot nectar	500 mL
1 cup	water	250 mL
pinch	cinnamon	pinch
1 1/2 cups	quick-cooking (not instant) rolled oats	375 mL
1	ripe banana, mashed	1

In saucepan, bring nectar, water and cinnamon to a boil over medium heat. Stir in oats. Return to a boil. Reduce heat to medium-low and cook for 1 minute. Stir in banana until smooth.

Makes 4 servings.

Per serving: cal 236, pro 6 g, fat 3 g, carb 49 g, fibre 5 g

Tasty Tidbit

Did you know that both oatmeal and bananas contain soluble fibre? This fibre may help control diarrhea, as well as blood sugar levels and cholesterol.

Chicken Broth

An old-fashioned recipe designed to provide comfort. Add steamed white rice, boiled noodles and/or pieces of cooked chicken to the soup for a nutritious meal. This soup can be frozen in individual portions.

4	chicken leg quarters	4
12 cups	cold water	3 L
2	carrots, cut into 2-inch (5 cm) chunks	2
2	stalks celery, cut into 2-inch (5 cm) chunks	2
1	small onion, quartered	1
1/2 cup	fresh parsley or thyme	125 mL
1 tbsp	salt	15 mL

In large soup pot or saucepan, pour water over chicken. Bring to a boil.

Remove scum with spoon. Add carrots, celery, onion, parsley and salt. Cover and return to a boil. Reduce heat and simmer for 3 hours, occasionally removing scum.

Strain soup through a large sieve or colander into a large container. Cool broth to room temperature, then cover and refrigerate. Remove skin and bones from chicken and shred meat. Save for soup or other use. Discard vegetables.

Remove solidified layer of fat on top of broth. Pour broth into individual containers and freeze for another time.

Makes 12 servings.

Per serving (1 cup/250 mL): cal 39, pro 5 g, fat 1 g, carb 1 g, fibre 0 g

Tasty Tidbit

Homemade chicken soup is the ultimate comfort food, recommended by grandmothers worldwide. Try adding rice or pasta to make a heartier, more filling soup. To increase your protein, chop the cooked chicken into small pieces and add to the soup.

Broth-Based Soup Ideas

Ever increasing ranges of broth – vegetable, chicken and beef – are available making it simple to make a nourishing bowl of soup. Tetra Pak broths are particularly convenient; just use straight from the carton. Canned broths generally require diluting with an equal amount of water. Dry cube or sachet broths are reconstituted with boiling water. Just be aware that many of these can be quite salty.

Stracciatella Soup (Version 2)

1	egg	1
1 tsp	grated Parmesan or Romano cheese, optional	5 mL
1 tsp	minced parsley, optional	5 mL
	salt and pepper to taste	
1 cup	broth	250 mL

In small bowl, beat egg with cheese, parsley, salt and pepper. Set aside.

In small saucepan, bring broth to a boil.

Slowly pour egg mixture into boiling broth and gently stir so that egg mixture breaks up into pieces.

Once egg mixture is completely cooked, remove from heat.

Makes about 2 servings.

Per serving (3/4 cup/175 mL): cal 41, pro 4 g, fat 2 g, carb 1 g, fibre 0 g

Tips
• Try these tasty variations:
  – Add small size pasta such as pastina, orzo or rice noodles to simmering broth. Cook until pasta is tender.
  – Add cooked plain white rice to simmering broth.
  – Add chopped cooked chicken or beef to simmering broth.
  – Add chopped extra-firm tofu to a simmering vegetable broth.

Tasty Tidbit
Stracciatella means "little shreds". This soup was first made in Rome. The name comes from beaten eggs gently stirred into hot broth. The egg in this soup provides a source of protein.

CHICKEN RICE CONGEE

Congee is rice soup, common in China.

1/2 cup	long grain rice	125 mL
6 cups	chicken broth, canned or homemade	1.5 L
1 - 2 cups	diced cooked chicken or turkey	250 - 500 mL

In medium saucepan, stir together rice and broth. Bring to a boil, reduce heat to low, cover and simmer for 1 hour. Add chicken and simmer 1 hour longer or until soup has thickened.

Makes 4 servings.

Per serving: cal 209, pro 19 g, fat 5 g, carb 20 g, fibre 0 g

TIP
• If using condensed chicken broth, dilute according to package directions.

TASTY TIDBIT
Traditionally a Chinese breakfast food known as *hsi-fan* or rice water, this simple rice soup is easy to digest. Any combination of your favourite ground or diced cooked meats can be added for flavour and heartiness.

CRISPY CHICKEN FINGERS

Chicken fingers make a tasty light supper or an appetizer. Serve with plum sauce, sweet mango chutney or other favourite dipping sauce. Cooked in a skillet, these are quick and crispy.

1	package (300 g) chicken fillets	1
1	egg	1
3 tbsp	milk	45 mL
1/2 cup	fine dry bread crumbs	125 mL
1 tsp	paprika	5 mL
1/2 tsp	each, salt, dried thyme, dried oregano and dried parsley flakes	2 mL
2 tsp	vegetable oil	10 mL

In shallow bowl, lightly beat egg and blend in milk.

In pie plate or other shallow plate, combine bread crumbs and seasonings with a fork until well blended.

Cut off the white tendon at the top of each fillet with kitchen shears or sharp knife. Rinse fillets under cold water and pat dry. Dip chicken pieces in egg mixture then roll in crumbs until evenly coated. Place on wax paper as they are coated.

Add vegetable oil to a large nonstick skillet and spread oil evenly over bottom of pan with a brush or paper towel. Heat pan over medium heat. When warm, lightly brown 5 or 6 chicken fingers at a time for 4 to 5 minutes per side. Do not crowd pan.

Makes 11 to 12 fingers.

Per serving (4 fingers): cal 242, pro 28 g, fat 7 g, carb 14 g, fibre 1 g

TIP
• Substitute 300 g chicken cutlets or 2 boneless, skinless chicken breasts (with fillets removed). Cut lengthwise into 3- x 1-inch (8 x 2.5 cm) strips.

TASTY TIDBIT
You can substitute the bread crumbs in this recipe with crushed Corn Flakes® as a tasty alternative. Crushed Corn Flakes® are available ready-made in the supermarket.

SIMPLE CHICKEN POT PIE

Substitute 2 cups (500 mL) mashed potatoes (made with margarine and/or lactose-free milk) for the toast topping, if desired. Add some sliced cooked carrots or green beans to chicken mixture for colour, flavour and variety.

2 tbsp	all-purpose flour	25 mL
3/4 cup	chicken broth, canned or homemade	175 mL
1 cup	diced cooked chicken or turkey	250 mL
3 - 4	slices white bread, cubed	3 - 4

In small saucepan whisk flour into chicken broth until smooth. Bring to boil, stirring constantly. Reduce heat to low and continue to stir until thickened, about 1 minute.

Stir chicken into sauce and spoon into a lightly greased 3-cup (750 mL) baking dish or casserole. Place bread cubes on top. Broil for 2 to 3 minutes or until bread is toasted.

Makes 2 servings.

Per serving: cal 294, pro 27 g, fat 7 g, carb 28 g, fibre 1 g

TASTY TIDBIT
Did you know that pot pies in Northern Europe were made in a pot lined with crust? This crust was not eaten but was there to keep the taste of the iron pot away from the food. By the time the pot pie crossed the Atlantic the pastry bottom flipped to the top. This made it easier to hang above a fire to cook.

Chicken, Rice and Mushroom Sauté

This can also be made with leftover cooked chicken or turkey. Just add it near the end with the asparagus to heat through. Green or yellow beans can be used in place of the asparagus.

1 tbsp	vegetable oil	15 mL
1/2 lb	boneless, skinless chicken thighs or breasts, cut into 1-inch (2.5 cm) pieces	250 g
1 cup	sliced mushrooms	250 mL
1 cup	long grain rice	250 mL
2 cups	chicken broth	500 mL
1/2 tsp	dried thyme	2 mL
4	asparagus spears, cut into 1-inch (2.5 cm) pieces	4
	salt and pepper	

In large saucepan, heat oil over medium heat. Add chicken and cook a few minutes to lightly brown meat.

Add mushrooms and rice and cook 1 minute, stirring constantly. Stir in broth and thyme and bring to a boil. Reduce heat and simmer, covered for 15 minutes, stirring occasionally.

Stir in asparagus and cook until rice is tender, liquid is absorbed and asparagus is cooked, about 5 minutes. Season to taste with salt and pepper.

Makes 4 servings.

Per serving: cal 293, pro 17 g, fat 7 g, carb 38 g, fibre 1 g

Tip
• It's a snap to prepare asparagus. Clean well, then snap off ends – they will snap naturally where the tough part begins.

Tasty Tidbit
In North America, asparagus is freshest and most affordable during the spring. When buying asparagus, look for thicker stems as they are more flavourful.

Turkey and Vegetable Loaf

This can also be made with half lean ground beef and half turkey or chicken.

1 tsp	vegetable oil	5 mL
1/2 cup	diced mushrooms	125 mL
1/2 cup	diced green pepper	125 mL
1 lb	lean ground turkey or chicken	500 g
1	small potato, peeled and grated	1
1	small carrot, grated	1
1/4 cup	chicken broth	50 mL
1/2 tsp	salt	2 mL
1/4 tsp	dried thyme	1 mL
1/4 tsp	dried basil	1 mL
1/4 cup	oatmeal (rolled or quick-cooking, not instant)	50 mL
1/4 cup	tomato sauce	50 mL

Heat oil in small skillet over medium-high heat and sauté mushrooms and pepper until lightly softened (or microwave in a bowl for 3 minutes on high).

Combine turkey with vegetables, broth, salt, thyme, basil and oatmeal. Place in a lightly greased 9- x 5-inch (2 L) loaf pan. Spread tomato sauce evenly over top.

Bake in preheated 375°F (190°C) for 45 minutes or until well done (no longer pink in centre).

Makes 6 servings.

Per serving: cal 153, pro 17 g, fat 5 g, carb 10 g, fibre 1 g

Tasty Tidbit
Turkey is a delicious, nutritious alternative to chicken or red meat. Ground turkey can be used to replace ground beef in many recipes and is available in most supermarkets.

Veal Scaloppini with Mushrooms

Thin pork or chicken cutlets can be used in place of veal. Serve with pasta or potatoes.

1 lb	thinly sliced veal cutlets	500 g
	salt, pepper, paprika	
1 tbsp	canola oil	15 mL
1/4 cup	apple juice	50 mL
1 tsp	lemon juice	5 mL
1/2 lb	fresh mushrooms, sliced	250 g
2 tbsp	chicken broth or bouillon	25 mL
2 tsp	chopped fresh parsley	10 mL

Season veal slices with salt and pepper. Sprinkle lightly with paprika on both sides.

In large skillet over medium heat, heat oil. Cook veal, in batches as necessary, until lightly browned on both sides. Set veal aside and keep warm.

Pour apple and lemon juices into skillet and bring to a simmer. Add mushrooms and cook until tender, about 10 minutes.

Add chicken broth to skillet and boil one minute. Spoon mushroom sauce over veal slices and garnish with parsley.

Makes 4 servings.

Per serving: cal 173, pro 25 g, fat 6 g, carb 4 g, fibre 1 g

Tip
- For small amount of chicken broth or bouillon use liquid chicken concentrate, cubes or sachets diluted as per label.

Tasty Tidbit
Did you know that the two main types of parsley are called flat-leafed (also known as Italian) and curly-leafed? Fresh parsley can be stored in the refrigerator with the stems in a glass of water.

LEMONY BAKED FISH

1 lb	cod, sole or other white fish fillets	500 g
	salt and pepper	
1 tbsp	melted butter or margarine	15 mL
1 tbsp	lemon juice	15 mL
1 tsp	dried dill weed or 2 tbsp (25 mL) chopped fresh dill	5 mL

Arrange fish in single layer in a lightly greased baking dish. Season with salt and pepper.

Combine melted butter, lemon juice and dill; pour over fish. Bake in preheated 425°F (220°C) oven for approximately 10 minutes or until fish flakes when tested with a fork.

Makes 4 servings.

Per serving: cal 120, pro 20 g, fat 4 g, carb 0 g, fibre 0 g

TASTY TIDBIT

Fresh dill is a wonderful addition to many fish dishes. For a simple fish sauce try mixing fresh dill, low-fat yogurt and a squeeze of lemon.

Easy Pretzel-Style Buns

Fresh or frozen dough can be bought in any grocery store. Pretzels may be frozen after baking.

1	package (700 - 750 g) refrigerated or frozen pizza or bread dough	1
1	egg, lightly beaten	1
1 tbsp	water	15 mL
	coarse salt	

If using frozen dough, allow to thaw in refrigerator. With sharp knife, cut dough into 12 pieces. Roll each piece into a 12-inch (30 cm) rope. Shape each rope into a pretzel. Place pretzels on greased baking sheets.

Let rise 20 minutes.

Whisk egg with water. With a pastry brush, brush pretzels with egg wash; sprinkle with salt.

Bake in preheated 350°F (180°C) oven for 20 minutes, or until golden brown.

Makes 12 pretzels.

Per pretzel: cal 151, pro 4 g, fat 4 g, carb 24 g, fibre 1 g

Tips
- Purchased bread and pizza dough can vary in size. A 450 g package will make about 8 pretzels.
- To make mini buns, cut dough into 24 pieces. Shape into sticks or circles like a donut. Follow directions above, baking 18 minutes, until golden brown. Makes 24.
- If dough sticks to hands or counter, lightly flour hands before rolling dough.

Tasty Tidbit
Did you know that pretzels have been enjoyed for over a thousand years? Legend has it that a European monk used leftover bread dough and baked them as treats.

OVEN-BAKED POTATO WEDGES

1	medium baking potato, peeled	1
1 tsp	vegetable oil	5 mL
	salt and pepper	

Cut potato into wedges. Toss with oil and salt and pepper to taste.

Place on shallow rimmed baking sheet lined with parchment paper or aluminum foil. Bake in preheated 400°F (200°C) oven for 20 to 30 minutes or until crisp and golden outside and tender inside. Turn or flip potatoes partway through cooking.

Makes 1 serving.

Per serving: cal 185, pro 3 g, fat 5 g, carb 34 g, fibre 3 g

TASTY TIDBIT
The part of the potato plant we eat is called the tuber, which is actually an enlarged underground stem. Originally from Peru, it is one of the best loved foods in the world. It is also a great source of potassium.

Carrots with Zip

Cooked carrots are easily tolerated.

18 - 20	baby carrots	18 - 20
1 tsp	cornstarch	5 mL
1//4 tsp	ground ginger	1 mL
1/4 cup	pulp-free orange or apple juice	50 mL

Cook carrots in boiling, lightly salted water until tender-crisp, about 10 minutes. Drain.

In medium saucepan, whisk together cornstarch, ginger and orange juice. Bring to a boil over medium heat. Reduce heat to low and simmer 2 minutes. Stir in carrots and cook until heated through.

Makes 2 servings.

Per serving: cal 54, pro 1 g, fat 1 g, carb 12 g, fibre 2 g

Tasty Tidbit
Carrots are one of the sweetest and most popular root vegetables. Did you know that some nutrients in carrots are better absorbed when the carrots are cooked?

Banana Yogurt Cookie Delight

This is a very easy make-ahead dessert.

36	vanilla flavoured wafers	36
2	bananas, cut in 1/2-inch (1 cm) slices	2
2	containers (175 g) of low-fat vanilla, peach or plain yogurt	2
1/4 tsp	cinnamon or nutmeg	1 mL

Line bottom of 8-inch (2 L) square baking dish with crumbled wafers. Arrange bananas evenly over crumbs. Spoon yogurt evenly over bananas. Sprinkle with cinnamon or nutmeg. Cover with plastic wrap and refrigerate overnight.

Makes 8 servings.

Per serving: cal 133, pro 3 g, fat 4 g, carb 23 g, fibre 1 g

Tips
- If using a fruit-bottom yogurt, stir well before using. Substitute lactose-free yogurt if you are unable to tolerate regular yogurt.
- Arrowroot cookies, social tea cookies or lemon wafers can also be used for the crumb crust.

Tasty Tidbit
Did you know that you can buy yogurt containing active bacteria? This may be easier to digest than milk if you have diarrhea.

LACTOSE-FREE BAKED CUSTARD

2 1/2 cups	lactose-free 2% milk	625 mL
3	eggs	3
1/3 cup	granulated sugar	75 mL
1 tsp	vanilla	5 mL
	ground nutmeg, optional	

In a glass bowl, heat milk in microwave oven on medium for 2 to 3 minutes or until warm.

In large bowl, whisk together eggs, sugar, and vanilla until blended. Add milk and stir until thoroughly combined. Pour mixture into six 6-oz (175 mL) ramekins or custard cups. Sprinkle with nutmeg, if using.

Place cups in a 13- x 9-inch (3.5 L) baking pan. Pour enough hot tap water into pan to come halfway up ramekins. Bake in preheated 350°F (180°C) oven for 40 minutes or until a knife inserted in the centre comes out clean. Remove from water and cool on wire rack. Serve warm or chilled.

Makes 6 servings.

Per serving: cal 128, pro 6 g, fat 4 g, carb 15 g, fibre 0 g

Lactose-Free Bread Pudding

Add 2 cups (500 mL) day-old bread cubes to warm milk and let stand 5 minutes to soften. Add eggs, sugar and vanilla and stir well. Pour into a greased 6-cup (1.5 L) casserole. As above, place casserole in large pan with hot tap water and bake at 350°F (180°C) for 60 minutes or until knife inserted in centre comes out clean. Serve warm or cold.

Makes 8 servings.

Per serving: cal 119, pro 6 g, fat 4 g, carb 16 g, fibre 0 g

Tasty Tidbit

Vanilla pods *(vanilla planifolla)* are actually from the orchid family. Originally used as a perfume because of its distinctive aroma, vanilla is now available as a liquid extract or in its original pod, where the seeds are scraped off and used for their flavour.

Lactose-Free Rice Pudding

1/2 cup	water	125 mL
1/2 cup	instant rice	125 mL
1 3/4 cups	lactose-free 2% milk	425 mL
2 tbsp	granulated sugar	25 mL
1/4 tsp	salt	1 mL
1	egg	1
1 tsp	vanilla	5 mL
1/2 tsp	nutmeg or cinnamon	2 mL

In saucepan, bring water to a boil and stir in rice. Remove from heat, cover and let stand 5 minutes.

Stir in milk, sugar and salt and bring to a boil over medium heat, stirring constantly. Reduce heat and simmer, uncovered for 5 minutes, stirring occasionally.

In bowl, whisk egg, vanilla and nutmeg together. Gradually stir a small amount of hot rice mixture into beaten egg, mixing well. Blend egg mixture into hot rice in saucepan. Cook and stir over low heat for 1 minute. Do not boil. Remove from heat and immediately pour into dessert dishes or serving bowl. When using lactose-free milk, place a layer of plastic wrap directly on the surface of the pudding to prevent a skin from forming.

Makes 4 servings.

Per serving (1/2 cup/125 mL): cal 146, pro 6 g, fat 3 g, carb 22 g, fibre 0 g

Tip

• To heat a leftover serving of cold rice pudding, simply microwave on medium for 20 to 30 seconds.

Tasty Tidbit

This nutritious pudding may be used as a tasty snack or dessert. It's a good source of protein and calcium.

Soy Pudding

Puddings are so easy to make in the microwave — no worry about scorched pots or burnt milk.

1/4 cup	granulated sugar	50 mL
2 tbsp	cornstarch	25 mL
1 1/4 cups	vanilla or strawberry soy beverage	300 mL
1 tsp	vanilla	5 mL

In a 4-cup (1 L) microwavable bowl, combine sugar and cornstarch. Gradually whisk in soy beverage until smooth. Microwave uncovered on high for 3 to 4 minutes, whisking twice during cooking, until mixture comes to a boil and thickens.

Whisk in vanilla until blended and pour into three 6-oz (175 mL) ramekins or custard cups. Serve warm or chill until set, about 2 hours.

Makes 3 servings.

Per serving: cal 155, pro 3 g, fat 2 g, carb 27 g, fibre 1 g

Tasty Tidbit

Did you know that some soy beverages are fortified with calcium? If you are looking to increase your calcium intake, check the label on your soy beverage.

Mango Ice

Cold foods that are soft in texture and sweet in taste are easily tolerated. Take the mango out of the freezer 20 minutes before making the ice.

2 cups	frozen mango chunks	500 mL
1 1/2 cups	water	375 mL
1/2 cup	honey	125 mL
2 tbsp	lemon juice	25 mL

In blender or food processor, purée mango, water, honey and lemon juice until smooth. Pour into plastic or glass bowl or container and freeze for 6 hours or until firm.

Remove from freezer about 15 minutes before serving. Scoop with an ice cream scoop. Use within 5 days.

Makes about 8 servings.

Per serving (1/2 cup/125 mL): cal 92, pro 0 g, fat 0 g, carb 25 g, fibre 1 g

Tip
• To use granulated sugar instead of honey, use 2/3 cup (175 mL) sugar and stir into water until sugar is dissolved before combining with remaining ingredients.

Tasty Tidbit
Did you know that mangoes are consumed ten times more than apples worldwide? Mangoes are a great source of vitamin A and vitamin C.

BANANA BREAD

This bread can be sliced and frozen in individual portions.

1 cup	mashed ripe bananas (2 medium)	250 mL
1 tsp	baking soda	5 mL
1/2 cup	plain low-fat yogurt	125 mL
1/4 cup	vegetable oil	50 mL
1/2 cup	brown sugar	125 mL
1	egg, beaten	1
1 tsp	vanilla	5 mL
1 1/2 cups	all-purpose flour	375 mL
1 tsp	baking powder	5 mL
pinch	salt	pinch

In small bowl combine bananas, baking soda, and yogurt. Set aside. In large bowl combine oil, sugar, egg and vanilla, blend well. Add banana mixture and blend.

In small bowl stir together flour, baking powder, and salt. Add to banana mixture and stir until just moistened.

Spread batter into a lightly oiled 8- x 4-inch (1.5 L) loaf pan. Bake in preheated 350°F (180°C) oven for 50 to 60 minutes or until loaf springs back when gently touched. Let cool in pan on rack for 15 minutes. Turn out onto rack; let cool completely.

Makes 1 loaf, 12 slices.

Per slice: cal 162, pro 3 g, fat 5 g, carb 26 g, fibre 1 g

TIP
• When you have an abundance of brown speckled ripe bananas, freeze without peeling. When ready to use, thaw and mash.

TASTY TIDBIT
Banana bread recipes are known as "quick breads" – breads leavened with baking powder. They can easily be made into muffins. Just reduce the baking time. You'll know they are ready when a skewer, toothpick or cake tester inserted into the muffin comes out clean!

CHAPTER 6

Getting Back *on* Track

The information in this chapter focuses on the return to a healthier diet now that some of the eating difficulties experienced during the treatment process are starting to subside.

During treatment, your dietary goals were to maintain strength, stamina and hydration. The focus was on lots of calories for energy, enough protein for healing and fluid to keep you well hydrated. Depending on the type or types of side effects you experienced, your diet may have been very limited. In certain situations, some important foods or food components were removed because it could have made your symptoms worse. For instance, when experiencing diarrhea, it might have been suggested to avoid high-fibre foods like dried peas and beans.

The return to a regular diet will be gradual as side effects begin to diminish. Keep in mind that the rate at which side effects improve will differ for everyone. The type of treatment and response to treatment is specific to your body. Use this as a guide to find the best approach for you.

LOWER YOUR FAT INTAKE

Many people may have increased fat intake as a way to maintain weight during treatment. They just could not eat enough. Since fat has more than double the calories per gram than protein or carbohydrate, it is an easy way to increase energy.

When your appetite is better, you will likely be able to eat more. If weight loss is no longer a problem and you are happy at your present weight, it is a good time to reduce the extra fat added to the diet. This will limit unwanted weight gain now that you are eating more foods.

SIMPLE WAYS TO DECREASE FAT INTAKE

1. Choose lower-fat dairy products.
   - Add skim or 1% milk to cereal instead of whole milk.
   - Check labels on cheese; choose products that have less than 17% milk fat (MF).
   - Have low-fat yogurt (less than 2% MF) for a snack instead of ice cream.
   - Use 2% milk in cream soup recipes instead of cream.
   - Skip the whipped cream on desserts or coffee.

2. Choose leaner meats.
   - Look for extra lean ground beef, chicken or turkey for meatloaf recipes.
   - Trim the fat off meat and remove the skin from poultry before cooking.

3. Use less butter, margarine, oils and gravy.
    - Consider whether you need the extra pat of butter or margarine on your toast in the morning or your mashed potatoes at dinner.
    - Have gravy on the side instead of on top of meat and potatoes. This way you can control the amount.

4. Limit or replace high-fat, high-calorie snack foods.
    - Have pretzels instead of chips.
    - Munch on fresh fruit or vegetables with low-fat dip.
    - Have popcorn plain instead of smothered in butter.

CHOOSING BETTER FATS

High intake of saturated fats has been linked to an increased risk of certain diseases.

Saturated fats are found in meat, poultry and dairy foods as well as coconut oil, palm oil, palm kernel oil and shortening. Using leaner meats and lower-fat dairy products can help you cut down on saturated fat intake while maintaining protein and other essential nutrient intake.

Hydrogenated fats are fats that have undergone a chemical process to make them easier to use. For instance, it is much simpler to spread margarine on toast than it is to spread oil. However, this process results in the formation of trans fats that may be harmful. Most processed foods, commercially baked goods, fast foods and margarine contain trans fats. Reading nutrition labels and ingredient lists will help you cut down on these fats. Avoid products that have *hydrogenated fat*, *partially hydrogenated fat, trans fatty acids* and/or *trans fat* on the label. Look for ingredients like *non-hydrogenated fat* or *oil* on the package.

Unsaturated fats have been found to be better for your health. They can be divided into 2 categories: monounsaturated fats (MUFA) and polyunsaturated fats (PUFA). Sources of MUFA are canola oil, olive oil, avocados, and nuts like peanuts and almonds. Sources of PUFA are corn oil, safflower oil, soybean oil, sunflower oil and most seafood. Omega-3 fat is a PUFA that has been found to have many health benefits of its own. Good sources of omega-3 fat are ground flax seed or flax oil, black walnuts, omega-3 eggs, wheat germ or wheat germ oil, canola oil and soy oil. Fatty fish like salmon, mackerel, herring, sardines, albacore tuna, halibut, striped bass and cod are also great sources of omega-3 fat.

Although these fats are considered to be better, it is still important to limit their use. Only small amounts are necessary for the diet especially when weight loss is no longer a concern.

ADD FIBRE BACK INTO YOUR DIET

When dealing with any of the side effects discussed throughout the book, fibre may have been reduced or eliminated from the diet. If you had a sore mouth, foods that are high in fibre may have been difficult to chew. If you experienced diarrhea, you may have been told to avoid certain foods with fibre because they could not be properly digested.

Now that your symptoms have improved, you can gradually add fibre back into the diet. It is important to start slowly so that your body can get used to the extra fibre. Depending on how you feel, you can try to add one or two suggestions on a weekly basis. How quickly you add fibre into the diet may also be based on how severe your side effects were. Remember also to keep your fluid intake up. Your body needs extra fluid when you add fibre to the diet. Aim for 6 to 8 (8-ounce/250 mL) glasses per day.

SIMPLE WAYS TO INCREASE FIBRE INTAKE

1. Choose whole-grain breads, cereals, pasta, rice and flour.
   - Add a tablespoon (15 mL) of an all-bran cereal to your usual breakfast cereal.
   - Have a bran muffin instead of a tea biscuit.
   - Use whole-wheat bread for a sandwich instead of white bread.
   - Switch from white rice to brown rice.
   - Switch from regular pasta to whole-wheat pasta.
   - Substitute half of the white flour called for in recipes with whole-wheat flour. You may need to increase the amount of liquid used.

2. Increase your intake of fruits and vegetables.
   - Have an apple instead of apple juice.
   - Eat a baked potato *with* the skin instead of mashed potatoes.
   - Add raisins or dried apricots to bread or muffin recipes.
   - Top ice cream with fruit compote or a scoop of berries.

3. Include legumes (otherwise known as dried peas and beans) and nuts as protein sources in the diet. Legumes may be gassy and hard to digest – add them last to the diet and start with a small serving.
   - Add a tablespoon (15 mL) of nuts to cereal or yogurt.
   - Snack on trail mix instead of potato chips.
   - Add kidney beans to your favourite chili recipe.
   - Use hummus as a dip instead of salsa.
   - Add canned beans to salads.

When you are ready to add legumes to the diet, here are some ways to reduce gas:

- For canned beans, drain the liquid and rinse beans well before using.
- For dried peas and beans, soak them overnight. The next day discard soaking water and rinse beans well. Cook in fresh water.
- Cook dried beans thoroughly. This makes them more easily digested.
- For soups with legumes, purée the final product before serving.

FOCUS ON VEGETABLES AND FRUIT

For one reason or another your vegetable and fruit intake may have been low during treatment. It could have been related to the side effects you experienced or a general lack of appetite. As you begin to feel better, look at expanding your diet to include more vegetables and fruit. Start slowly and gradually work up to 5 to 10 servings per day.

One serving of fruit or vegetable is equivalent to:

- 1 medium size vegetable or fruit (about the size of a tennis ball)
- 1/2 cup (125 mL) of chopped vegetable or fruit
- 1 cup (250 mL) of salad
- 1/2 cup (125 mL) of juice
- 1/4 cup (50 mL) of dried fruit

SIMPLE WAYS TO INCREASE VEGETABLES AND FRUIT

1. Include vegetables and fruit from each of these colour groups. Each colour indicates the presence of a different type of nutrient.
    - Green – broccoli, green beans, peas, leafy greens, honeydew, kiwi fruit, green grapes
    - Orange/yellow – carrots, squash, sweet potato, oranges, nectarines, mango, papaya
    - Red – tomatoes, red peppers, strawberries, pink grapefruit, cherries, watermelon
    - Blue/purple – eggplant, purple grapes, plums, blueberries, purple figs, black currants
    - White – cauliflower, mushrooms, onions, garlic, turnips, bananas, pears, apples

2. Experiment with new varieties and unfamiliar vegetables and fruit. This way you do not miss out on any specific nutrients they may contain.
   - Each time you go to the grocery store, add a new type of vegetable or fruit to your cart.
   - Be adventurous at a restaurant and try an entrée or dessert that contains unfamiliar vegetables or exotic fruits.

3. Add one or two choices to meals and snacks. This is an excellent way to cut down on fat and add fibre to the diet too.
   - Top your cereal with bananas and raisins.
   - Snack on vegetables and low-fat dip.
   - Have a fruit smoothie.
   - Enjoy a salad or vegetable soup at the start of the meal.
   - Include vegetables in a spaghetti sauce or chili recipe.
   - End your meal with fruit or if you crave dessert – top it with fruit.

PUTTING IT ALL TOGETHER

This information will help you get back on track with your diet. Remember to start slowly and focus on one or two changes at one time. It may be helpful to record your intake for a few days. This way you can note whether or not you experience any problems with the changes. It can also highlight what you are doing well and what needs to be improved.

Here are some examples of what you might notice when keeping a food record.
1. Your fruit intake is good *BUT* you need to eat more vegetables.
2. Your fibre intake is great at breakfast *BUT* not at lunch and dinner.
3. You manage to eat low-fat foods at home *BUT* when you eat out everything you order is high-fat.

This chapter provides you with the basics to get started. There are a number of other resources available that can assist you on your road to recovery. Here is a list of reliable and helpful books and websites that may be of interest.

BOOKLETS

Eat Well, Be Active – What you can do
   by the Canadian Cancer Society

COOKBOOKS

Healthy Home Cooking
  by Margaret Howard

Anne Lindsay's New Light Cooking
Anne Lindsay's Light Kitchen
Lighthearted Everyday Cooking
The Lighthearted Cookbook
Smart Cooking
  by Anne Lindsay

Eat Well, Live Well
  by Helen Bishop MacDonald and Margaret Howard

Low-Calorie Cajun Cooking
  by Enola Prudhomme

High-Flavour Low-Fat Cooking
  by Steven Raichlen

Rose Reisman's Enlightened Home Cooking
Rose Reisman Brings Home Light Cooking
Rose Reisman Brings Home Light Pasta
  by Rose Reisman

More Vitality Cookbook
The Vitality Cookbook
  by Monda Rosenberg and Frances Berkoff

New Low-Fat Favourites
Low Fat and Loving It
  by Ruth Spear

More Heartsmart Cooking
Simply Heartsmart Cooking
  by Bonnie Stern

The Cancer Survival Cookbook: 200 Quick and Easy Recipes with Helpful Eating Hints
  by Donna L. Weihofen and Christina Marino

MealLeaniYumm!
  by Norene Gilletz

VEGETARIAN COOKING

Full of Beans
by Violet Curry and Kay Spicer

Cooking Vegetarian
by Vesanto Melina and Joseph Forrest

Rose Reisman's Light Vegetarian Cooking
by Rose Reisman

SOY

The Whole Soy Cookbook
by Patricia Greenberg

FLAX

A Taste of Flax. The Cookbook.
by the Flax Council of Canada; Tel: 204-982-2115; Fax: 204-942-1841

KOSHER LOW-FAT COOKING

Secrets of Fat-Free Kosher Cooking
by Deborah Bernstein

WEBSITES

Dietitians of Canada
www.dietitians.ca

Canadian Cancer Society
www.cancer.ca

Health Canada
www.hc-sc.gc.ca

5 to 10 a day for Better Health
www.5to10aday.com

Canadian Health Network
www.canadian-health-network.ca

American Dietetic Association
www.eatright.org

American Institute for Cancer Research
www.aicr.org

APPENDIX I – WHERE TO FIND INGREDIENTS

Ingredient	"Where to Find It…" Section
Applesauce, unsweetened	Baking or canned fruit
Apricots, dried	Produce (with nuts)
Baking powder	Baking
Baking soda	Baking
Banana chips, dried	Produce (with nuts)
Beans, red kidney	Canned vegetables
Beans, white	Canned vegetables
Berries, frozen	Freezer
Bread crumbs	Fresh bakery
Bread dough, frozen	Freezer
Bread dough, refrigerated	Fresh bakery
Buttermilk	Dairy
Chickpeas	Canned vegetables
Chocolate cookie crumbs/Chocolate cookie crumb crust	Baking
Chocolate wafers	Cookie
Coconut, shredded	Baking
Corn syrup	Pancake mix
Cornstarch	Baking
Cottage cheese	Dairy
Couscous	Rice
Cranberries, fresh	Produce
Cranberries, frozen	Freezer
Cream of Wheat® cereal, quick	Cereal
Dates	Baking or Produce
Edamame, frozen	Freezer
Fish	Freezer or fish counter
Garlic, bottled	Condiments or produce
Gelatin, unflavoured	Baking
Graham cracker crumbs/Graham crumb crust	Baking
Green tea bags	Tea and coffee

Ingredient	"Where to Find It…" Section
Herbs and spices, dried – basil, chili powder, cinnamon, cumin, curry powder, dill, dillweed, ginger (ground), Italian seasoning, mustard (dry), nutmeg, oregano, paprika, parsley flakes, rosemary, tarragon, thyme, turmeric	Spice
Herbs and seasonings, fresh – cilantro, coriander leaves, dill, ginger, mint leaves, parsley, rosemary, thyme	Produce
Hoisin sauce	Condiments
Hot pepper sauce	Condiments
Jelly powders	Baking
Ladyfingers	Fresh bakery
Lemon juice	Juice
Lentils, red, dried	Canned vegetables
Lime juice	Juice
Mango chunks, frozen	Freezer
Mango chutney	Condiments
Meringue powder	Fresh bakery, bulk food stores, or cake decorating stores
Milk, lactose-free	Dairy
Mustard, Dijon	Condiments
Nectar – apricot, mango, peach	Juice
Parmesan cheese, grated	Pasta
Peach slices, frozen	Freezer
Peanut sauce	Condiments
Pecans, chopped	Baking
Pita	Fresh bakery
Pizza dough, frozen	Freezer
Pizza dough, refrigerated	Fresh bakery
Pizza sauce	With tomato sauces
Powdered drink mix	Juice
Pumpkin purée, cooked	Baking
Raisins	Baking or Produce
Red wine vinegar	Salad dressing
Roasted red pepper, bottled or canned	With olives and pickles
Rolled oats, quick cooking	Cereal
Romano cheese, grated	Pasta

Ingredient	"Where to Find It..." Section
Rum extract	Baking
Skim milk powder	Baking
Soy beverage	Dairy
Soy sauce	Condiments
Spinach, frozen	Freezer
Sponge cake shells	Fresh bakery
Sunflower seeds, shelled	Produce (with nuts)
Teriyaki sauce	Condiments
Tofu – firm, soft, silken	Produce
Tortilla	Fresh bakery
Vanilla	Baking
Vanilla wafers	Baking or cookie
Whipped topping, frozen	Freezer
Yogurt, lactose-free	Organic dairy

APPENDIX II – HOW TO STOCK YOUR PANTRY

Stocking your pantry with these items will make it easier to prepare meals or to find a snack when hunger strikes. You may want to use this as a guide when writing your shopping list as well.

CUPBOARD

CANNED AND BOTTLED GOODS

- Applesauce, individual portions
- Beans and peas – black beans, chick peas, kidney beans
- Broth – beef, chicken, vegetable
- Frosting
- Fruit cocktail, individual portions
- Peaches, individual portions
- Pudding, individual portions
- Salmon
- Soup – broth-based, cream
- Spaghetti sauce
- Tomato paste
- Tomatoes, peeled
- Tuna, light

DRY GOODS

- Baking powder
- Baking soda
- Beans and peas – lentils, pinto beans, split peas
- Boullion cubes or sachets – beef, chicken, vegetable
- Bread crumbs
- Bread sticks
- Cake mixes
- Cereal, cold
- Cereal, hot (instant) – Cream of Wheat®, oatmeal
- Crackers
- Flour – white, whole wheat
- Fruit – apricots, banana chips, raisins
- Gelatin

- Herbs and spices – basil, bay leaves, cinnamon, ginger, nutmeg, oregano, pepper, rosemary, salt, thyme
- Jelly powder desserts
- Melba toast
- Nuts – almonds, cashews, peanuts, pecans, walnuts
- Pasta – orzo, shells, spaghetti, tubes
- Pudding mixes
- Rice – brown, instant, white, wild
- Rice cakes
- Salad dressing mixes
- Seeds – pumpkin, sesame, sunflower
- Skim milk powder
- Sugar – brown, white

MISCELLANEOUS

- Garlic
- Oil – olive, canola
- Onions
- Potatoes
- Vinegar – balsamic, cider, wine

REFRIGERATOR

- Barbeque sauce
- Butter
- Cheese slices
- Chicken or turkey, sliced
- Cottage cheese
- Eggs
- Honey
- Jams and jellies
- Maple syrup
- Margarine, non-hydrogenated
- Mayonnaise
- Milk
- Molasses
- Mustard

- Nectar drinks
- Peanut butter and other nut butters
- Pickles
- Relish
- Salad dressing
- Soy beverage
- Soy sauce
- Yogurt
- Yogurt drinks

FREEZER

- Bagels
- Bread
- Buns
- Burgers – beef, turkey, soy
- Chicken breasts, boneless, individual portion
- English muffins
- Entrées, frozen
- Fish fillets, frozen
- Fruit, frozen
- Ice cream
- Pancakes, frozen
- Pitas
- Pizza dough or crusts, frozen
- Pizza, individual, frozen
- Popsicles
- Sherbet
- Vegetables, frozen
- Waffles, frozen
- Yogurt, frozen

The food suggestions listed above are general recommendations. They do not take into account side effect management. For specific information, refer to the chapter introduction for each side effect. For storage tips, refer to Appendix IV – *Food Safety*.

APPENDIX III – WHAT IS A HEALTHY DIET?

A healthy diet is one that provides you with the essential nutrients your body needs to function properly, to fight infection and to reduce the risk of developing nutrition-related problems. It can also contribute to an overall sense of wellbeing.

Government agencies such as Health Canada and health organizations such as the Canadian Diabetes Association (CDA), the American Heart Association (AHA) and the American Institute for Cancer Research (AICR) all provide guidelines for a healthy diet. These are based on research in the field of nutrition and in the prevention of specific diseases.

It can become confusing when looking at the many different suggestions for a healthy diet. Fortunately, when the recommendations from credible sources are pooled together, the similarities in their messages can be seen.

For instance, if we combine the guidelines from Health Canada, the United States Department of Agriculture (USDA), the Department of Health and Human Services (HHS) and AICR, we see the following key messages:

1. Consume a VARIETY of foods.

2. Choose a diet rich in PLANT-BASED foods.

3. Choose fats wisely. Choose LEANER meats. Choose LOWER-FAT dairy products.

4. Choose carbohydrates wisely. Emphasize WHOLE GRAINS and FIBRE-rich grains.

5. Eat plenty of VEGETABLES and FRUITS.

6. Choose and prepare foods with LITTLE SALT.

7. Drink alcohol only in MODERATION, if at all.

8. Achieve and maintain a HEALTHY BODY WEIGHT by enjoying regular physical activity and controlling calorie intake.

PUTTING THEORY INTO PRACTICE

The tool nutrition professionals refer to most often when educating about a healthy diet is their nation's food guide. Food guides can vary slightly from country to country, but the main message is similar. In Canada, it is "Canada's Food Guide to Healthy Eating" and in the United States, it is "MyPyramid," previously the Food Guide Pyramid.

Another tool that has gained popularity is the plate model. AICR's version is "The New American Plate." The plate model is a simple way to show appropriate portions of foods at meals. It is easy to use at home or when dining out. It includes many key nutrition strategies.

Here is how you would build a healthy plate:

Start with vegetables. They are an excellent source of fibre and nutrients, and are low in calories. They should make up 1/2 of your plate. Possibilities are a salad or a stir-fry. Aim for at least 2 different colours of vegetables on your plate and don't forget to experiment with the unfamiliar.

Then add your starchy foods. Choose whole-grain and high-fibre types such as brown rice, whole-wheat pasta, potato with the skin, a multigrain roll, etc. Starchy foods are naturally higher in calories than vegetables and should make up only about 1/4 of the plate. Another method you can use to determine portion size is your hand. A good portion of grains is equal to the size of an average fist. Remember this when dining out at your favourite Mediterranean restaurant.

Protein foods provide essential nutrients, especially important in times of recovery from illness. Great sources of protein include lean meats and poultry, omega-3 rich fish, low-fat dairy products, tofu, and legumes such as lentils and kidney beans. Limiting protein to 1/4 of the plate helps with weight control but ensures you still get its benefits. Other measures you can use to determine one serving of protein are the palm of your hand or a deck of cards.

To complete the meal, add fresh fruit. Fruit is an excellent source of fibre, vitamins and minerals. To improve your chances of getting different types of nutrients, break the habit of "an apple a day." Try something new and go for colour. One serving of fruit is about the same size as a tennis ball.

WHERE TO GO FOR MORE INFORMATION

Health Canada
for Canada's Food Guide to Healthy Eating
www.hc-sc.gc.ca/fn-an/index_e.html

Public Health Agency of Canada (PHAC)
for Canada's Guide to Healthy Eating and Physical Activity
www.phac-aspc.gc.ca

United States Department of Agriculture (USDA)
for MyPyramid: Steps for a Healthier You
www.MyPyramid.gov

American Institute of Cancer Research (AICR)
for The New American Plate
www.aicr.org

APPENDIX IV – FOOD SAFETY

Food-borne illness, also known as food poisoning, occurs often. Many people do not know they have food poisoning because its symptoms resemble the flu. Both illnesses can present with stomach cramps, nausea, vomiting, diarrhea and/or fever. During cancer treatment, the immune system that usually protects you from infection may be weakened. There is a greater chance that you may develop a serious illness from eating contaminated food.

Contamination of food is caused by improper storage, cooking or handling. Bacteria, viruses, moulds, fungi and parasites can also be found naturally in food. Unfortunately, you cannot always tell if food is spoiled by how it looks, smells or tastes. If you are not sure about its safety, it is best to just throw it out!

This may sound scary, but food safety can be easy when you know which foods to avoid and how to cook, store and handle food properly. This chapter will provide basic guidelines for keeping food safe.

SHOPPING

Safe eating begins with the food you buy. Remember to put refrigerated and frozen foods into your shopping cart last. This will limit the amount of time that food is sitting at room temperature.

- Buy packages that are properly sealed and cans with no dents, bulges, cracks or leaks. Avoid buying products from open bins and foods that are displayed without a package. Examples are bulk food items, unwrapped bakery products and items from the deli counter.
- Do not buy more than a 1-week supply of raw fruits and vegetables. Avoid buying fruits and vegetables that are bruised, damaged or overly ripe. Do not buy raw vegetable sprouts such as alfalfa sprouts, bean sprouts and clover sprouts.
- Buy juice and cider that is pasteurized.
- Do not buy meat that is displayed raw, unwrapped and touching other raw or cooked meats. Limit cross-contamination by placing meat, poultry and fish in plastic bags. Instruct the checkout clerk to place these items in separate bags from ready-to-eat foods and fresh produce.
- Buy eggs that are refrigerated and have no cracks.
- Buy only pasteurized, refrigerated milk and dairy products.
- Make sure frozen foods are solid and there are no ice crystals formed on the outside of the package. This may be a sign that the food was thawed and refrozen.
- Always check "best before" dates. Choose dates that are far into the future. Examples of food with a "best before" date are milk, cheese and eggs.

- The "packaged on" date is the day the food was wrapped. For instance, raw meat will have a date stamped on its package. This date should be the day of your shopping trip and not a day or two before.

STORAGE

Foods that require refrigeration or freezing should be stored as soon as you return home from grocery shopping. Do not leave them at room temperature. Do not store any food supplies under the kitchen sink.
- Label frozen food with the date of purchase or preparation.
- Dry goods, once opened, should be reclosed before storing.
- Remember to rotate food so the older items are used first.
- Do not let raw foods touch ready-to-eat foods.

The Danger Zone

Bacteria multiply very quickly between 40°F (4°C) and 140°F (60°C). This is known as the danger zone. Always keep refrigerated foods cold – at or below 40°F (4°C). This will inhibit the growth of bacteria. Always keep hot food hot – at or above 140°F (60°C).

PREPARATION

- Wash your hands for at least 20 seconds. Use liquid or pump soap and warm, running water. Dry hands on a clean towel that is used only for that purpose. This is one of the best ways to limit contamination of food and the spread of illness. Don't forget to wash your hands after using the washroom, taking out the garbage or touching your pet!
- Wash your hands properly before and after each step in food preparation. This is most important before and after handling raw meat, poultry and seafood.
- Keep your work area clean at all times – especially during food preparation. Use hot, soapy water to clean dishes, utensils, can openers and inside the microwave. This will reduce the chance of cross-contamination.
- Wipe dust or dirt off the lids of canned goods with a clean, damp towel before opening. Do not use cans that spurt when opened, appear bubbly or have a bad smell.
- It is a good idea to use at least 3 separate cutting boards. One for cooked foods, one for vegetables and one for raw meat, poultry, fish and seafood. After each use, wash the boards with hot, soapy water then rinse with hot water and let dry thoroughly. Boards used for raw meat, poultry, fish and seafood must be disinfected with a bleach solution and rinsed with hot water after each use. Plastic cutting boards can be cleaned in the dishwasher.

- Wash fruits and vegetables thoroughly under cold, running water before peeling or cutting. Scrub produce that has a thick, rough skin or has dirt on the surface with a clean vegetable scrubber. Throw out the outside leaves of leafy vegetables and wash each inside leaf separately. Rinse packaged and prepared produce even if it is marked "pre-washed." Do not use soap as this can be absorbed into the produce.
- Use a clean utensil each time food is tasted during preparation. Do not taste foods that contain raw eggs until cooked.

COOKING

- Place frozen meat on a tray to thaw on the bottom shelf of the refrigerator. Do not let it drip on other foods, especially ready-to-eat foods. Never thaw food at room temperature.
- Use a food thermometer to make sure food is cooked to a safe internal temperature. Look, texture and colour are not reliable methods to determine if the food item is cooked properly.
- Poultry should not be stuffed. Cooking stuffing separately in its own dish ensures that the different internal temperatures of the bird and the stuffing can be reached.
- Eggs should be cooked until the white and yolk are completely firm.
- Use different plates and utensils for raw food and cooked foods.

Food Item	Safe Internal Temperature	
	°C	°F
Beef/veal steaks, roasts – Medium	71	160
– Well done	77	170
Pork chop, ribs, roasts Ground beef/ground pork/ground veal Sausages made with ground beef/pork/veal	71	160
Ground chicken/ground turkey Sausages made with ground chicken/turkey	74	165
Chicken/turkey – breasts, legs, thighs, wings Chicken/turkey – whole bird, unstuffed	85	185
Fish	70	158
Egg dishes, casseroles, hot dogs, leftovers	74	165
Stuffing – cooked separate from chicken and turkey	74	165

Adapted from Canadian Food Inspection Agency "When is my food ready to eat?"

WHAT TO DO WITH LEFTOVERS

- Place in a covered container and refrigerate right away.
- If there are large amounts left over, divide into small, shallow containers first. This will make sure the food cools down quickly. Then cover containers.
- If you do not plan to eat leftovers within 2 to 3 days, place in the freezer instead.
- Reheat soups, stews and sauces thoroughly. Stir frequently. Make sure that the temperature reaches 165°F (74°C) throughout.
- Throw out food that has been sitting at room temperature for more than 2 hours. If it is a hot summer day, throw it out after 1 hour.
- Leftover canned food should be transferred to a glass or plastic container. Then, the container should be covered, labelled, refrigerated and used within a few days.

TAKING FOOD TO A FRIEND

Home-cooked foods can be very comforting for someone who is sick. Ask your friend if there is something she or he would like you to make. If there is, here are some guidelines to help you keep the food safe.

- Cook food and divide among single-serving containers. Refrigerate or freeze the item immediately. Make sure to label it with the date.
- When you are ready to leave your home, pack the food in a cooler with an icepack for the trip. Once you arrive at your friend's home, reheat fully in the microwave oven following the guidelines for microwave cooking.
- If your friend is not hungry when you arrive, store the food in the refrigerator. If he or she does not plan to eat the item in the next 2 to 3 days, it is safer to store it in the freezer.
- For immediate use, you can use an insulated thermal container for hot foods, such as soups and stews.

KITCHEN CLEAN-UP

- Throw out foods that have been in the freezer for more than 3 months.
- Throw out cooked or leftover foods that have been in the refrigerator for more than 2 or 3 days.
- Throw out raw fruits and vegetables that are slimy or are starting to show mould.
- Throw out food that has mould on it. Don't take a chance!
- Throw out food that has an expired "best before" date.

- Canned food may not have an expiration date but throw them out if you have had them for more than 1 year.
- Throw out canned goods that have dents, bulges, cracks or leaks. Don't taste it first!

- Change hand towels daily or as needed throughout the day.
- Replace dishcloths daily or as needed throughout the day.
- Wash and sanitize hand towels and dishcloths. Use the hot cycle of the washing machine.
- Wash cutting boards after each use. Use hot, soapy water then rinse with hot water and let dry thoroughly.
- Disinfect cutting boards used for raw meat, poultry, fish and seafood after each use. Use a bleach solution then rinse with hot water and let dry thoroughly.
- Replace cutting boards when deep grooves in the surface make cleaning difficult.
- Use a pump or liquid soap for hand washing.
- Clean the inside of the refrigerator weekly.
- Clean any spills immediately whether in the refrigerator, in the freezer, on the counter or on the floor.
- Keep appliances free of food particles including crumbs.

- Place working thermometers in your refrigerator and freezer.
- Check temperatures regularly.
- Refrigerator temperature – at or below 40°F (4°C)
- Freezer temperature – at or below 0°F (-18°C)

BLEACH SOLUTION		
3 tbsp	unscented household bleach	45 mL
4 cups	water	1 L

Mix bleach with water. Store in a spray bottle. Make sure it is clearly labelled!
Keep it in a handy place away from food, children and pets.

NEED MORE INFORMATION?

There are a lot of education materials available on food safety. For more specific information you can check out any of the following reliable resources. It is important to know that some regulations vary from one country to another. An example of this is safe internal temperatures for food.

Canadian Partnership for Consumer Food Safety Education
www.canfightbac.org

Fight Bac! Partnership for Food Safety Education
www.fightbac.org

Canadian Health Network
www.canadian-health-network.ca

Canadian Food Inspection Agency
www.inspection.gc.ca

Food Safety Information Society
www.foodsafetyline.org
Toll free 1-800-892-8333

Health Protection and Promotion Branch, Ontario Regulation # 562 – Food Handling
www.e-laws.gov.on.ca

United States Department of Agriculture (USDA) Food Safety and Inspection Service
www.fsis.usda.gov

It is important to drink lots of fluids even if you are not feeling well and your appetite is poor. Try to drink *at least* 8 cups (2 L) of fluid each day. Keep in mind the amount you need depends on your body size and/or the side effects of your treatment. You may need extra fluids to prevent dehydration if you are experiencing diarrhea, vomiting or have a fever. To help you increase your fluids, try some of the choices and tips listed below.

GOOD FLUID CHOICES

- Water
- Vegetable and fruit juices
- Broth-based soups
- Weak tea, decaffeinated tea or decaffeinated coffee
- JELL-O®, or store-brand jelly desserts
- Popsicles
- Ice cubes
- Caffeine-free soft drinks
- Fruit-flavoured drinks such as Kool Aid®, Tang®, etc.
- Sports drinks such as Gatorade® or Powerade®, etc.

GOOD FLUID CHOICES WITH CALORIES AND PROTEIN TOO

These fluids are great to use if you need to drink more and need to gain weight. If you have diarrhea, you may want to limit your intake of these fluids. For more information, see introduction to Chapter 5 – *Dealing with Diarrhea*.

- Milk (2%, homogenized or chocolate)
- Milkshakes or smoothies
- Hot chocolate
- Soy beverage
- Nutrition supplements such as Ensure®, Boost®, Resource®etc.
- Carnation Breakfast Anytime®, etc.
- Ice cream
- Frozen yogurt
- Sherbet or sorbet
- Yogurt or yogurt drinks
- Cream soups

HOW TO KEEP HYDRATED

- Sip fluids throughout the day.
- Carry something to drink with you when you go out.
- Limit intake of caffeine or alcohol-containing fluids.
- Make an effort to drink even if you are not thirsty.
- Consider drinking liquids between meals if you find you get full quickly at meal times.
- If you are only able to drink 1 cup (250 mL) of fluid during the day, try to gradually increase your intake by 1 cup (250 mL) more each day. By the end of the week, you will be very close to meeting your needs.

How to Find a Registered Dietitian

A registered dietitian (R.D., R.D.N., P.Dt., or Dt.P.) is a health professional with an accredited undergraduate university degree in foods and nutrition or equivalent and an accredited internship/practicum or equivalent.

Most cancer treatment centres have registered dietitians as part of the health care team who can provide individualized counselling about diet during and after treatment. If you have any nutritional concerns, ask your doctor, nurse or radiation therapist for a referral.

If you are no longer being followed at a cancer centre, ask your family doctor for a referral to a dietitian in your area. There may be a registered dietitian in your local community health centre or public health unit.

Here are some places that you can contact for a registered dietitian near you.

Dietitians of Canada
www.dietitians.ca
416-596-0857

L'Ordre Professionnel des Diététistes du Québec (Quebec only)
www.opdq.org
1-888-393-8528

Dial-a-Dietitian (British Columbia only)
www.dialadietitian.org
604-732-9191 in Greater Vancouver area
1-800-667-3438 outside Greater Vancouver area

American Dietetic Association
www.eatright.org

Glossary

Allergy – A condition of having a hypersensitive reaction to a certain substance. These reactions can range from mild to life-threatening.

Antioxidant – A nutrient that can protect the body's cells from damage by removing oxygen by-products.

Appetite – A desire for food.

Baste – To moisten food while cooking so that the surface does not dry out. Liquids usually used are melted fat, drippings, sauces and fruit juices. They also add flavour.

Boil – To cook in a liquid that is heated to the point where bubbles are continually forming.

Broil – To cook food under direct heat, usually on a rack in an oven.

Caffeine – A mild stimulant found in coffee, tea and cocoa, and added to some soft drinks and medications.

Cake tester – A thin utensil, often metal, used to check doneness of baked goods. The tester is inserted into centre of cake and indicates that the cake is done if it comes out dry. Toothpicks are often used for this purpose.

Calcium – A mineral important in bone health. It is found in milk and dairy products, fortified soy products, fortified orange juice and canned salmon and sardines.

Calorie – A unit of measure to show the energy value of food. Carbohydrate, protein, fat and alcohol contain calories.

Carbohydrate – A sugar or a starch. Foods that contain carbohydrates include grains (like wheat, rice and corn), vegetables, legumes, milk products, fruit, as well as sugar-based products like candy, jam and regular soft drinks.

Coat – To dip food into flour, a sauce, etc. until it is covered.

Colander – A container with many small holes used to wash or drain foods; a sieve.

Cross-contamination – The transfer of harmful bacteria from one food product to another. This is a common cause of food poisoning. It is most important to keep raw meat, poultry, seafood and their juices away from cooked foods and ready-to-eat foods.

Dehydration – A condition in which a person's body has too little water. This is caused by not drinking enough fluid and/or by fluid losses through uncontrolled vomiting or diarrhea.

Drain – To pour off liquid, often using a strainer.

Dredge – To cover or coat a food completely, often with flour.

Drizzle – To pour a small amount of liquid onto a food.

Dust – To sprinkle with a powdery substance, like icing sugar.

Enriched – A term indicating that nutrients (usually vitamins or minerals) lost during processing have been added back to the food. An example is the enrichment of white flour with B vitamins. The B vitamins are lost when the wheat is refined.

Fat – The most concentrated form of calories or energy. Oil is fat in liquid form, and contains the same amount of energy. See Chapter 6 – *Getting Back on Track – Choosing Better Fats* for a discussion of these types of fat:

- Polyunsaturated fat
- Omega-3 fats (also known as Omega-3 fatty acids)
- Monounsaturated fat
- Saturated fat
- Hydrogenated fat

Fibre – The indigestible component of unrefined carbohydrate foods. Fibre has many beneficial functions, such as adding bulk and helping to regulate blood glucose and cholesterol, but can be difficult to tolerate at times during treatment.

Fold in – To combine delicate ingredients with other foods by using a gentle, circular motion to cut down into the mixture, slide across the bottom of the bowl to bring some of the mixture up and over the surface.

Food-borne illness – See Appendix IV – *Food Safety*

Food poisoning – See Appendix IV – *Food Safety*

Fortified – A term indicating that a nutrient (usually a vitamin or mineral) has been added to a food that was not present originally. An example is milk which is fortified with vitamin D.

Garnish – To decorate a dish with a small amount of food, often parsley, croutons or chopped vegetables.

Gluten – A protein found in cereal grains – specifically wheat, rye, barley and oats.

Grazing – The practice of eating a small amount many times during the day, rather than eating three large meals. This technique helps people with small appetites to consume more overall.

Grill – To cook food over direct heat usually on a rack.

Iron – A mineral important for the health of the blood and immune system. It is found in organ meats, red meat, poultry, eggs, legumes and fortified cereals.

Knead – To work a ball of dough by hand. Dough is kneaded by repeatedly folding over, pressing down and turning.

Lactose-intolerance – A condition in which a person is not able to digest the natural sugar in milk (lactose). Symptoms include cramping, bloating, gas and diarrhea.

Legumes – Plants having seeds growing in pods. They are sources of protein and fibre. Examples of legumes are lentils, kidney beans and chickpeas.

Lukewarm – Mildly warm.

Lutein – An antioxidant important in eye health. It is found in egg yolk, corn, spinach and other fruits and vegetables.

Lycopene – An antioxidant important in heart and prostate health. It is a red pigment found mainly in tomatoes and tomato products, and is absorbed better when cooked in oil or fat. Other sources include watermelon, red grapefruit and guava.

Magnesium – A mineral important for the immune system and bone health. It is found in whole grains, green vegetables, legumes, almonds and cashews.

Marinade – A liquid used to soak food in for flavouring and moistening before cooking. Always marinate foods in the refrigerator. If a marinade is used for raw meat, fish or poultry, it must be discarded after removing the raw food, because it can be a source of food poisoning if it comes in contact with other food. See "cross-contamination."

Milk
• Homogenized milk – also referred to as "whole milk" – contains 3.5% milk fat
• Skim milk – also referred to as "fat-free" or "nonfat" milk
• 1% milk – also referred to as "low-fat" milk
• 2% milk – also referred to as "reduced-fat" milk

Mould – A hollow form for shaping a liquid as it sets.

Nutrient – A substance that provides nourishment.

Osteoporosis – A condition in which bones become fragile due to calcium loss.

Parchment paper – A heavy, grease- and moisture-resistant paper, often used for lining baking pans.

Pasteurize – The process of using heat to kill bacteria. Common pasteurized foods are milk and juice.

Pastry blender – A cooking utensil with U-shaped wires attached to a handle. It is used to cut a cold fat (usually butter) into dry ingredients to distribute fat without warming it.

Potassium – A mineral important for muscle and nerve function as well as the regulation of fluids in the body and blood pressure. It is found in many fruits and vegetables, including bananas, potatoes, tomatoes and orange juice.

Preheat – To heat an oven to the temperature in the recipe before putting the food in it.

Protein – Food that contains amino acids, which are necessary for building muscle, blood, skin and organs. Sources of protein are meat, poultry, fish, eggs, dairy products, legumes and nuts.

Purée – To blend or rub through a strainer until smooth.

Ramekin – A small, individual baking dish.

Rise – To puff up, become larger.

Roast – To cook uncovered in an oven.

Saucepan – A deep cooking pan with a handle.

Sauté – To fry quickly in a small amount of fat, stirring often.

Sieve – A utensil with many small holes to strain liquids or fine particles; a colander.

Skewer – A long, fine utensil, used to pierce and hold small pieces of food for grilling.

Skillet – A frying pan.

Soy beverage – A drink made from soybeans, often used as a milk substitute by vegetarians or people with a milk allergy or lactose-intolerance.

Spatula – A utensil with a flat, broad, flexible blade for spreading or flipping food.

Spring-loaded ice cream scoop – A scoop with an inset movable bar to make dispensing ice cream easier.

Steam – To cook food on a rack in a covered pan above lightly boiling water.

Strain – To squeeze out liquid from food.

Tofu – Soybean curd. It is a protein source, commonly used in Asian and vegetarian cooking.

Vitamin A – A vitamin important in eye health. It is found in milk, eggs, liver and fortified cereals.

Vitamin C – A vitamin important in wound healing. It is found in many fruits and vegetables, including citrus fruit, tomatoes, strawberries and bell peppers.

Vitamin D – A vitamin important in bone health. It is found in fortified milk, fish, and fortified cereals.

Vitamin E – A vitamin important in protecting cells. It is found in vegetable oils, wheat germ, nuts and fortified cereals.

Whisk – A quick stirring motion to blend foods smoothly or to whip air into a mixture. Also the name of the cooking utensil made for this purpose.

Zest – The outer peel of a lemon, orange or other citrus fruit, used as flavouring.